D. A Compton, Pierr Blot

The Prize Essay on the Cultivation of the Potato

D. A Compton, Pierr Blot

The Prize Essay on the Cultivation of the Potato

ISBN/EAN: 9783744786577

Printed in Europe, USA, Canada, Australia, Japan

Cover: Foto ©Andreas Hilbeck / pixelio.de

More available books at **www.hansebooks.com**

THE

PRIZE ESSAY

ON THE

CULTIVATION OF THE POTATO.

Prize offered by W. T. WYLIE and awarded to D. H. COMPTON.

HOW TO COOK THE POTATO,

Furnished by Prof. BLOT.

ILLUSTRATED. PRICE, 25 CENTS.

New-York:

ORANGE JUDD CO.,

No. 245 BROADWAY.

PRIZE ESSAY

ON THE

POTATO AND ITS CULTIVATION.

$100.

In the fall of 1868, I offered $100 as a prize for the best Essay on the Cultivation of the Potato, under conditions then published ; the prize to be awarded by a committee composed of the following gentlemen, well known in agricultural circles :

Colonel MASON C. WELD, Associate Editor of *American Agriculturist*.

A. S. FULLER, Esq., of Ridgewood, N. J., the popular author of several horticultural works, and Associate Editor of the *Hearth and Home*.

Dr. F. M. HEXAMER, who has made the cultivation of the potato a special study.

In the month of January, 1870, the committee awarded the prize to D. A. Compton ; and this Essay is herewith submitted to the public in the hope of stimulating a more intelligent and successful cultivation of the Potato.

BELLEFONTE, PA., January, 1870.   W. T. WYLIE.

POTATO CULTURE.

BY D. A. COMPTON, HAWLEY, PENNSYLVANIA.

THE design of this little treatise is to present, with minuteness of detail, that mode of culture which experience and observation have proved to be best adapted to the production of the Potato crop.

It is written by one who himself holds the plow, and who has, since his early youth, been engaged in agriculture in its various branches, to the exclusion of other pursuits.

The statements which appear in the following pages are based upon actual personal experience, and are the results of many experiments made to test as many theories.

Throughout the Northern States of our country the potato is the third of

OFFICE OF THE AMERICAN AGRICULTURIST, }
NEW-YORK, January, 1870.   }

REV. W. T. WYLIE: DEAR SIR : The essays submitted to us by Mr. Bliss, according to your announcement, numbered about twenty. Several could not be called essays from their brevity, and others were exceedingly incomplete. About twelve, however, required and were worthy of careful consideration. That of Mr. D. A. Compton, of Hawley, Wayne County, Pa., was, in the opinion of your committee, decidedly superior to the others as a practical treatise, sure to be of use to potato-growers in every part of the country, and well worthy the liberal prize offered by yourself.

In behalf of the committee, sincerely yours,   MASON C. WELD, *Chairman*.

the three staple articles of food. It is held in such universal esteem as to be regarded as nearly indispensable. This fact is sufficient to render a thorough knowledge of the best varieties for use, the character of soil best adapted to their growth, their cultivation and after-care, matters of the highest importance to the farmers of the United States.

The main object of this essay is so to instruct the novice in potato-growing that he may be enabled to go to work understandingly and produce the potato in its highest perfection, and realize from his labors bestowed on the crop the greatest possible profits.

SOIL REQUIRED—ITS PREPARATION.

The potato is most profitably grown in a warm, dry, sandy, or gravelly loam, well filled with decayed vegetable matters. The famous potato lands of Lake County, Ohio, from which such vast quantities of potatoes are shipped yearly, are yellow sand. This potato district is confined to ridges running parallel with Lake Erie, which, according to geological indications, have each at different periods defined its boundaries. This sand owes much of its potato-growing qualities to the sedimentary deposit of the lake and to manural properties furnished by the decomposition of the shells of water-snails, shell-fish, etc., that inhabited the waters.

New lands, or lands recently denuded of the forest, if sufficiently dry, produce tubers of the most excellent quality. Grown on dry, new land, the potato always cooks dry and mealy, and possesses an agreeable flavor and aroma, not to be attained in older soils. In no argillaceous soil can the potato be grown to perfection as regards quality. Large crops on

such soil may be obtained in favorable seasons, but the tubers are invariably coarse-fleshed and ill-flavored. To produce roots of the best quality, the ground must be dry, deep, and porous; and it should be remembered that, to obtain very large crops, it is almost impossible to get too much humus in the soil. Humus is usually added to arable land either by plowing under green crops, such as clover, buckwheat, peas, etc., or by drawing and working in muck obtained from swamps and low places.

The muck should be drawn to the field in fall or winter, and exposed in small heaps to the action of frost. In the following spring, sufficient lime should be mixed with it to neutralize the acid, (which is found in nearly all muck,) and the whole be spread evenly and worked into the surface with harrow or cultivator.

Leaves from the woods, buckwheat straw, bean, pea, and hop vines, etc., plowed under long enough before planting to allow them time to rot, are very beneficial. Sea-weed, when bountifully applied, and turned under early in the fall, has no superior as a manure for the potato. No stable or barn-yard manure should be applied to this crop. If such nitrogenous manure must be used on the soil, it is better to apply it to some other crop, to be followed the succeeding year by potatoes. The use of stable manure predisposes the tubers to rot; detracts very much from the desired flavor; besides, generally not more than one half as many bushels can be grown per acre as can be obtained by using manures of a different nature. Market gardeners, many of whom from necessity plant on the same ground year after year, often use fine old stable manure with profit. Usually they plant only the earlier varieties, crowd them with all possible speed, dig early, and sell large and little before they have time to rot, thus clearing the ground for later-growing vegetables. Thus grown, potatoes are of inferior quality, and the yield is not always satisfactory. Flavor, however, is seldom thought of by the hungry denizens of our cities, in their eagerness to get a taste of something fresh.

Market gardeners will find great benefit from the use of wood-ashes, lime, and the phosphates. Sprinkle superphosphate in the hill at the rate of two hundred pounds per acre; mix it slightly in the soil with an iron rake or potato-hook, then plant the seed. Just before the last hoeing, sprinkle on and around the hill a large handful of wood-ashes, or an equal quantity of lime slacked in brine as strong as salt will make it.

But for the generality of farmers, those who grow only their own supply, or those who produce largely for market, no other method of preparing the soil is so good, so easy, and so cheap as the following; it requires time, but pays a big interest: Seed down the ground to clover with wheat or oats. As soon as the grain is off, sow one hundred and fifty pounds of plaster (gypsum) per acre, and keep off all stock. The next spring, when the clover has made a growth of two inches, sow the same quantity of plaster again. About the tenth of July, harrow down the clover, driving the same direction and on the same sized lands you wish to plow; then plow the clover neatly under about seven inches deep. Harrow down the same way it was plowed, and immediately sow and harrow in two bushels of buckwheat per acre. When it has grown two inches, sow plaster as before; and when the buckwheat has grown as large as it will, harrow down and plow under about five inches deep. This, when cross-plowed in the spring sufficiently deep to bring up the

clover-sod, is potato ground *first-class in all respects.*

It is hardly supposable that this mode of preparation of soil would meet with favor among all farmers. There is a parsimonious class of cultivators who would consider it a downright loss of time, seed, and labor; but any one who will take the trouble to investigate, will find that these same parsimonious men never produced four hundred bushels of potatoes per acre; and that the few bushels of small tubers that they do dig from an acre, are produced at considerable loss. "Men do not gather grapes from thorns, nor figs from thistles."

To make potato-growing profitable in these times of high prices of land and labor, it is absolutely necessary that the soil be in every way fitted to meet any and all demands of the crop.

It is said that in the State of Maine, previous to the appearance of the potato disease, and before the soil had become exhausted by continued cropping, potatoes yielded an average of four hundred bushels per acre. Now, every observer is aware that the present average yield of the same vegetable is much less than half what it was formerly. This great deterioration in yield can not be attributed to "running out" of varieties; for varieties are extant which have not yet passed their prime. It can not be wholly due to disease; for disease does not occur in every season and in every place. True, we have more insects than formerly, but they can not be responsible for all the great falling off. It is traceable mainly to poverty of the soil in certain ingredients imperatively needed by the crop for its best development, and to the pernicious effect of enriching with nitrogenous manures. Any one who will plant on suitably dry soil, enriched only with forest-leaves, sea-weeds, or by plowing under green crops until the whole soil to a proper depth is completely filled with vegetable matter, will find to his satisfaction that the potato can yet be grown in all its pristine vigor and productiveness.

To realize from potato-growing the greatest possible profits, (and profits are what we are all after,) the following conditions must be strictly adhered to: First, the ground chosen *must be dry*, either naturally or made so by thorough drainage; a gently sloping, deep, sandy or gravelly loam is preferable. Second, the land should be liberally enriched with humus by some of the means mentioned, if it is not already present in the soil in sufficient quantities, and the soil should be deeply and thoroughly plowed, rendering it light, porous, and pulverulent, that the air and moisture may easily penetrate to any desirable depth of it; and a proper quantity of either wood-ashes or lime, or both, mixed with common salt, should be harrowed into the surface before planting, or be applied on top of the hills immediately after planting. And, finally, the cultivation and after-care should be *prompt*, and given as soon as needed. Nothing is more conducive to failure, after the crop is properly planted, than failure in promptness in the cultivation and care required.

GENERAL REMARKS ON MANURING WITH GREEN CROPS.

Experience proves that no better method can be adopted to bring up lands partially exhausted, which are remote from cities, than plowing under green crops. By this plan the farmer can take lot after lot, and soon bring all up to a high state of fertility. True, he gathers no crop for one year, but the outlay is little; and if in the second year he gathers as much from one acre as he formerly did from three, he is still largely the gainer.

It costs no more to cultivate an acre of rich, productive land than an acre of poor, unproductive land; and the pleasure and profit of harvesting a crop that abundantly rewards the husbandman for his care and labor are so overwhelmingly in favor of rich land as to need no comment. Besides, manuring with green crops is not transitory in its effects; the land remembers the generous treatment for many years, and if at times lime or ashes be added to assist decomposition, will continue to yield remunerative crops long after land but once treated with stable manure or guano fails to produce any thing but weeds. The skinning process, the taking off of every thing grown on the soil and returning nothing to it, is ruinous alike to farm and farmer. Thousands of acres can be found in various parts of the country too poor to pay for cultivating without manuring. Of the capabilities of their lands under proper treatment the owners thereof have no idea whatever. Such men say they can not make enough manure on the farm and are too poor to buy. Why not, then, commence plowing under green crops, the only manure within easy reach? If fifty acres can not be turned under the first year, put at least one acre under, which will help feed the rest. Why be contented with thirty bushels of corn per acre, when eighty or one hundred may be had? Why raise eight or twelve bushels of wheat per acre, when forty may as well be had? Why cut but one half-ton of hay per acre, when the laws of nature allow at least three? Why spend precious time digging only one hundred bushels of potatoes per acre, when with proper care and culture three or four hundred may easily be obtained? And, finally, why toil and sweat, and have the poor dumb beasts toil and sweat, cultivating thirty acres for the amount of produce that should grow, may grow, can grow, and has grown on ten acres?

The poorest, most forsaken side-hills, cobble-hills, and knolls, if the sand or gravel be of moderate depth, underlaid by a subsoil rather retentive, by turning under green crops grow potatoes of the first quality. If land be so poor that clover will not take, as is sometimes the case, seed to clover with millet very early in the spring, and harrow in with the millet thirty bushels of wood-ashes, or two hundred pounds of guano per acre; then sow the clover-seed one peck per acre; brush it in.

If neither ashes nor guano can be obtained at a reasonable price, sow two hundred pounds of gypsum per acre as soon as the bushing is completed. This will not fail in giving the clover a fair foothold on the soil.

Before the millet blossoms, cut and cure it for hay. Keep all stock off the clover, plaster it the following spring, plow it under when in full bloom; sow buckwheat immediately; when up, sow plaster; when in full bloom, plow under and sow the ground immediately with rye, to be plowed under the next May. Thus three crops are put under within a year, the ground is left strong, light, porous, free from weeds, ready to grow a large crop of potatoes, or almost any thing else.

Much is gained every way by having and keeping land in a high state of fertility. Some crops require so long a season for growth, that high condition of soil is absolutely necessary to carry them through to maturity in time to escape autumnal frosts. In the Western States manure has hitherto been considered of but little value. The soil of these States was originally very rich in humus. For a

time wheat was produced at the rate of forty bushels per acre; but according to the statistics given by the Agricultural Department at Washington, for the year 1866, the average yield in some of these States was but four and a half bushels per acre. It is evident from this that Mr. Skinflint has had things pretty much his own way. His land now produces four and a half bushels per acre; what time shall elapse when it shall be four and one half acres per bushel? Who dare predict that manure will not at some day be of value west of the Alleghanies? New-Jersey, with a soil naturally inferior to that of Illinois, contains extensive tracts that yearly yield over one hundred bushels of Indian corn per acre, while the average of the State is over forty-three; and the average yield of the same cereal in Illinois is but little over thirty-one bushels per acre. In the Western States, where potatoes are grown extensively for Southern markets, the average yield is about eighty bushels per acre; while in old Pennsylvania could be shown the last year potatoes yielding at the rate of six hundred and forty bushels per acre. There are those who argue that manure is never necessary—that plant-food is supplied in abundance by the atmosphere; it was also once said a certain man had taught his horse to live without eating; but it so happened that just as he got the animal perfectly schooled, it died.

Good, thorough cultivation and aeration of the soil undoubtedly do much toward the production of crops; but mere manipulation is not all that is needed.

That growing plants draw much nourishment from the atmosphere, and appropriate largely of its constituents in building up their tissue, is certainly true; it is also certainly true that they require something of the soil besides mere anchorage. All facts go to show that if the constituents needed by the plant from the soil are not present in the soil, the efforts of the plant toward proper development are abortive? What sane farmer expects to move a heavy load over a rugged road with a team so lean and poverty-stricken that they cast but a faint shadow? Yet is he much nearer sanity when he expects farming to be pleasant and profitable, and things to *move aright*, unless his land is strong and fat? Is he perfectly sane when he thinks he can skin his farm year after year, and not finally come to the bone? The farmer on exhausted land must of necessity use manure. Manure of *some* kind must go under, or he must go under; and to the great mass of cultivators no mode of enriching is so feasible, so cheap, and attended with such satisfactory results, as that of plowing under green crops.

The old plan of leaving an exhausted farm, and going West in search of rich "government land," must soon be abandoned. Already the head of the column of land-hunters have "fetched up" against the Pacific, and it is doubtful whether their anxious gaze will discover any desirable unoccupied soil over its waters.

The writer would not be understood as saying that all farms are exhausted, or that there is *no* way of recuperation but by plowing under green crops. What he wishes understood is, that where poor, sandy, or gravelly lands are found, which bring but small returns to the owner, by subjecting them to the process indicated, such lands bring good crops of the kind under consideration. And further, that land in the proper condition to yield a maximum crop of potatoes, is fitted to grow other crops equally well. Neither would the writer be understood as arguing that a crop of

clover and one of buckwheat should be turned under for each crop of potatoes; where land is already in high condition, it may not be necessary. A second growth of clover plowed under in the fall for planting early kinds, and a clean clover sod turned in *flat* furrows in the spring, for the late market varieties, answer very well. To turn flat furrows, take the furrow-slice wide enough to have it fall completely inside the preceding one.

Potatoes should not be planted year after year on the same ground; trouble with weeds and rapid deterioration of quality and quantity of tubers soon render the crop unprofitable. Loamy soil planted continuously soon becomes compact, heavy, and lifeless. Where of necessity potatoes must be grown yearly on the same soil, it is advisable to dig rather early, and bury the vines of each hill in the one last dug; then harrow level, and sow rye to be plowed under next planting time.

The intelligent farmer, who grows large crops for market, will always so arrange as to have a clover-sod on dry land in high condition each year, for potatoes. It is said by many, in regard to swine, that "the breed is in the trough;" though this is certainly untrue to a certain extent, yet it is undeniable that in potato-growing success or failure is in the character of soil chosen for their production.

Why clover, or clover and buckwheat lands, are so strongly urged is, such lands have in them just what the tubers need for their best and healthiest development; the soil is rendered so rich, light, and porous, and so free from weeds, that the cultivation of such land is rather a pleasure than otherwise, and at the close of the season the tangible profits in dollars and cents are highly gratifying.

VARIETIES.

From the fact that the United States produce about 109,000,000 bushels of potatoes annually, it might be supposed a great many varieties would be cultivated. Such, however, is not the fact. Of the varieties extant, comparatively few are grown extensively.

Every grower's observation has established the fact that for quality the early varieties are inferior to the late ones. The Early June is very early, but its quality is quite indifferent. The Cherry Blow is early, attains good size, and yields rather well. In quality it is poor. The Early Kidney, as to quality, is good, but will not yield enough to pay for cultivation. The Cowhorn, said to be the Mexican yam, is quite early, of first quality, but yields very poorly. The Michigan White Sprout is early, rather productive, and good. Jackson White is in quality quite good, is early, and a favorite in some places. The Monitor is rather early, yields large crops; but as its quality is below par, it brings a low price in market. Philbrick's Early White is one of the whitest-skinned and whitest-fleshed potatoes known. It is about as early as Early Goodrich, is quite productive, and grows to a large size, with but few small ones to the hill. Its quality is excellent. It has not yet been extensively tested. The Early Rose is said to be very early, of excellent quality, and to yield extremely well. It has, however, not been very widely tested. Perhaps for earliness and satisfactory product, the Early Goodrich has no superior. It is of fair quality, and though some seasons it does not yield as well as others, yet, all things considered, it is a desirable variety. The old Neshannock, or Mercer, is among the latest of the early varieties. As to quality, it is the standard of excellence of the whole potato family. But it yields rather poorly, and its liability to rot, except on soils especially fitted for it, has so discouraged growers that its cultivation in many sections is abandoned. On rather poor, sandy soil, manured in the hill with wood-ashes, common salt, and plaster only, it will produce in ordinary seasons two hundred bushels per acre of sound, merchantable tubers, that will always command the highest market price. Any potato cultivated for a long series of years will gradually become finer in texture and better in quality ; but its liability to disease will also be greatly increased. As an instance of this, it will be remembered that when the Merino and California varieties were first introduced, they were so coarse as to be thought fit only to feed hogs, and for this purpose, on account of their great yielding qualities, farmers continued to cultivate them, until finally they became so changed as in many sections to be preferred for the table. Their cultivation, however, is now nearly abandoned.

Of the later varieties, the Garnet Chili, a widely-diffused and well-known sort, deserves notice. It is not of so good quality as the Peach Blow ; but its freedom from disease, and the large crop it produces, make it a favorite with many growers. The chief fault with it is, the largest specimens are apt to be hollow at the centre. It ripens rather early; and, even when dug long before maturity, it has a dryness and mealiness, when prepared for the table, not found in many other sorts. The Buckeye is extensively grown for market ; its yield is not satisfactory, and its quality is only medium. The Dykeman is yet grown to some extent, but will soon be superseded.

The Prince Albert is a well-known and highly-esteemed variety, approaching very near the Peach Blow in quality. One peculiarity of this potato is, the largest tubers appear to be of as good quality as the small ones. With proper soil and culture, it yields a fair crop; is quite free from disease; and its smoothness, high flavor, and fine appearance make it much sought after in the market.

The Fluke, a very late potato, is a great favorite with many who produce for market. Its yield is very large; and its smoothness and uniformity of size make it altogether a desirable variety. It is generally free from disease. In quality it is rather above medium.

The Harrison, if it should do as well in the future as it has done in the past, bids fair to become *the* potato for general cultivation. It has yielded in this section, on soil of moderate fertility, with ordinary culture, one peck to the hill of uniform-sized, merchantable potatoes. It is a strong, vigorous grower, and very healthy. Its quality, though not the very best, is good. The Willard, lately originated by C. W. Gleason, of Massachusetts, is a half-early variety. It is enormously productive, of a rich rose color, spotted and splashed with white. The flesh is white. In form and size it closely resembles the Early Goodrich, its parent. It has not been extensively tested, but certainly promises well. The Excelsior is said, by those interested in its sale, to be very productive, and of most excellent quality, retaining its superior flavor all the year round. It is claimed that old potatoes of this variety are better than new ones of most early kinds, thus obviating the necessity of having early sorts. The Excelsior is said to cook very white and mealy; form nearly round, eyes prominent. It has not been much tested out of the neighborhood where it originated. But the potato-eater is yet unborn

who can justly find fault with a properly-grown Peach Blow. It is pronounced by many equal or superior to the Mercer in quality, which is not the fact. It is emphatically a late potato; and, though it does not yield as well per acre as some other sorts, it is comparatively healthy; and its quality is such that it always brings a high price in the market. In fact, but few other kinds of late sorts could find sale if enough of this kind were offered to supply the demand. Planted ever so early, it keeps green through the heat of summer, and never matures its tubers until after the fall rains, and then no potato does it more rapidly.

Grown on rich argillaceous soil, it will be hollow, coarse flesh, and ill-flavored; but planted on such soil as is recommended, it is about all that could be desired. It is a strong, vigorous grower; and one peculiarity of it is, that insects will not attack vines of this variety if other kinds are within reach.

Planted on extremely poor ground, it will, perhaps, yield more bushels of tubers, and those of better quality, than any other variety that could be planted on the same soil. Among all the old or new sorts, perhaps, no potato can be found that deteriorates so little in quality from maturity to maturity again. And, in fine, where only high quality with moderate yield are desired, it has few if any superiors.

Many other varieties might be mentioned; but the list given includes about all of much merit. New varieties are constantly arising, clamoring for public favor, many of which are wholly unworthy of general cultivation. One or two varieties, such as are adapted to the grower's locality and market, are preferable to a greater number of sorts grown merely for variety's sake.

INFLUENCE OF SOIL ON SEEDLINGS.

The characteristics of a potato, such as quality, productiveness, healthfulness, uniformity of size, etc., depend much on the nature of the soil on which it originated. These characteristics, some or all, imbibed by the minute potato from the ingredients of the soil, at its first growth from the seed of the potato-ball, adhere with great tenacity to it through all its generations. A seedling may, in size, color, and form resemble its parent; but its constitution and quality are in a great degree dependent on the nature of the soil, climatic influences, and other accidental causes.

True crosses are generally more vigorous and healthy than others; and it is probably to accidental crosses we are indebted for many varieties that differ so widely from their parents. A cross is most apparent to the eye when the parents are of different colors, in which case the offspring will be striped or marked with the colors of each parent.

HOW TO CROSS VARIETIES.

In order to comprehend fully the principles of this subject, and their application to practical operations, it will be necessary to take a general view of the generative organs of the vegetable kingdom, and the manner in which they act in the production of their species. If we examine a perfect flower, we shall find that it consists essentially of two sets of organs, one called the pistils, the other the stamens. The pistils are located in the centre of the flower, and the stamens around them. The summit of the pistil is called the stigma; and on the top of each stamen is situated an anther—a small sack, which contains the pollen, a dust-like substance, that fertilizes the ovules or young seeds of the plant.

These organs are supposed to perform offices analogous to those of the animal kingdom—the stamens representing the male, and the pistils the female organs.

When the anthers, which contain the pollen, arrive at maturity, they open and emit a multitude of minute grains of pollen; and these, falling on the pistils of the flower, throw out hair-like tubes, which penetrate through the vascular tissue of the pistil, and ultimately reach the ovules, thus fertilizing them, and making them capable, when mature, of reproducing plants of their own kind.

The ovules are the rudimentary seeds, situated in a case at the base of the pistils, each consisting of a central portion, called the nucleus, which is surrounded by two coats, the inner called the secundine, the outer the primine. When the hair-like tube of the pollen-grain passes through the orifice in the coatings of the ovule, and reaches the nucleus, or embryo sack, it is supposed to emit a spermatic or plantlet germ, which passes through the wall of the embryo sack and enters the germinal vesicle contained in it. The vesicle corresponds to the vesicle, or germinal spot, in the eggs of birds, and ovum of mammiferous animals. The germ remains in the vesicle, and finally becomes the embryo, fully developed into a plantlet, as may be seen in many seeds.

Flowers of plants are called perfect when the stamens and pistils are in the same flower, as the apple; monœcious, when in different flowers and on the same plant, as the white oak; and diœcious, when in different flowers and on different plants, as in the hemp. In that class of plants in which the stamens, or males, are on one plant, and the pistils, or females, on another, the males of course must always remain barren; and the pistilates, to be fruitful, must have the pollen from the anthers of the staminate brought in contact with its stigma by wind, insects, or other means. In plants with perfect flower, the stamens are generally situated around and above the pistil, so that the pollen falls upon the stigma by mere force of gravity. In the potato, the pollen is conveyed from the anthers to the stigma by actual contact of the two organs.

Cross-breeding in plants consists in fertilizing one variety with the pollen of another variety of the same species. The offspring is called a cross-breed, or variety. The process of cross-breeding consists in taking the pollen of one variety and applying it to the stigma of another variety, in such a way as to effect its fertilization. This is done by cutting away (with scissors) the stamens of the flower to be fertilized, a short time before they arrive at maturity, and taking a flower in which the pollen is ripe, dry, and powdery, from the stalk of the variety wished for the male parent; and holding it in the right hand, and then striking it on the finger of the left, held near the flower, thus scattering the pollen on the stigma of the pistil of the flower to be fertilized. The utmost care should be taken to apply the pollen when the flower is in its greatest vigor, and the stigma is covered with the necessary coating of mucus to insure a perfect connection of the pollen with the pistil, and make the fertilization perfect. All flowers not wanted in the experiment should be removed before any pollen is formed.

It is necessary to tie a thin piece of gauze over the flower to be fertilized, before and after crossing, to prevent insects from conveying pollen to it, thus frustrating the labors of the operator. If the operation has been successful, the pistil will soon begin to wither; if not perfect, the pistil will

continue fresh and full for some days. This *modus operandi* is substantially the same in crossing fruits, flowers, and vegetables throughout the vegetable kingdom.

Hybridizing differs from cross-breeding only in fertilizing one species, or one of its varieties, with the pollen of another species, or one of its varieties, of the same or a different *genus*. The offspring is called a hybrid, or mule. Hybrids, with very few exceptions, are sterile, they fail to propagate themselves from seed, and must, to preserve them, be propagated by grafts, layers, or suckers. No change is perceptible in the fruit produced from blossoms upon which the operation of cross-breeding or hybridizing has been performed ; but the seed of fruits so obtained may be planted with the certainty of producing a fruit or tuber commingling the qualities, colors, and main characteristics of both parents.

Experience, however, shows that the characteristics of the male predominate somewhat in the offspring. To judicious cross-breeding and hybridizing we owe most of our superior fruits and vegetables. If the operation were more generally known and practiced by farmers, the most gratifying results would be soon obtained, not only in the production of the most valuable varieties of potatoes and other vegetables, but also in fruits, flowers, and grain of every description.

SMOOTH VS. ROUGH POTATOES.

Other things being equal, smooth potatoes are preferable to those with deeply-sunken eyes. The starch being most abundant near the skin, not so much is lost by the thin paring of the former as by the necessarily deeper paring of the latter.

Varieties usually well formed sometimes grow so knobby and ill-shaped as to be scarcely recognized. This is caused by severe drought occurring when the tubers are about two thirds grown, causing them to partially ripen. On the return of moisture, a new growth takes place, which shows itself in knobby protuberances.

CUT AND UNCUT SEED.

Many growers argue that potatoes should be planted whole. The only plausible theory in support of whole seed is, that the few eyes that do start have a greater supply of starch available from which to obtain nutriment until the plant can draw support from the soil and atmosphere. But experiments also demonstrate that if all the eyes except one or two near the middle be cut out of the seed-potato, such seed will push with the greatest possible vigor.

Many eyes of the uncut seed start, but the stronger soon overpower the weaker, and finally starve them out. A plot planted with three small, uncut potatoes to the hill, and another planted with three pieces of two eyes each to the hill, will not show much difference in number of vines during the growing season.

The poor results sometimes attending cut seed are almost always traceable to improper seed improperly cut. Only large, mature, sound tubers should be used. Cut them in pieces of two or three eyes each, taking pains to secure around each eye as much flesh as possible, also under the eye to the centre of the tuber.

Experiments prove that eyes from the "seed end" produce potatoes that mature earliest; they are also smallest. Those from the large or stem end are largest, latest, and least in numbers. Eyes from the middle produce tubers of very uniform size.

If small, ill-shaped potatoes be planted on the same ground for three successive years, the results will give the best variety a bad name.

Much is gained by changing seed. No two varieties are made up of the same constituents exactly in the same proportion; hence, a soil may be exhausted for the best development of one, and still be fitted to meet the demands of another. Even when the same variety is desired, experience shows the great benefit of planting seed grown on a different soil. The best and most extensive growers procure new seed every two or three years, and many insist on changing seed every year; and undoubtedly the crop is often doubled by the practice.

PLANTING AND MANURING.

Early kinds should be planted as soon as the ground has become sufficiently dry and warm. Late market varieties should be planted about two weeks later than the early ones. Unquestionably more bushels can be obtained per acre by planting in drills than in hills, but the labor of cultivating in drills is much the greater.

Prepare the ground by thorough plowing, making it decidedly mellow. Mark it out four feet apart each way, if to be planted in hills, by plowing broad, flat-bottomed furrows about three inches deep. At the crossings drop three pieces of potato, cut, as directed, in sections of two or three eyes each. Place the pieces so as to represent the points of a triangle, each piece being about a foot distant from each of the other two. If the cut side is put down, it is better; cover about two inches deep. Where land is free from stone and sod, the covering may be well and rapidly done with a light plow. Immediately after planting, sprinkle over and around each hill a large handful of unleached wood-ashes and salt, (a half-bushel of fine salt mixed with a barrel of ashes is about the right proportion.) If ashes can not be obtained, as is sometimes the case, apply instead about the same quantity of lime slacked in brine as strong as salt will make it. The potato from its peculiar organization has a hungering and thirsting after potash. Wood-ashes exactly meet its wants in this direction. Lime indirectly supplies potash by liberating what was before inert in the soil. Salt in small quantities induces vigorous, healthy growth. To obtain the best results, the ashes or lime should be covered with about half an inch of soil. This plan of manuring in the hill is recommended only in cases where the fertilizers named are in limited supply, and it is desirable to make the most of them. Maximum crops have been obtained by using the fertilizers named in the manner described; but where they can be obtained at low prices, it is certainly advisable, and requires less labor, to apply all three, ashes, lime, and salt, broadcast in bountiful quantities, and harrow it in before the ground is marked out for planting.

CULTIVATION.

If weeds are expected, pass a light harrow over the rows just before the vines are ready to burst through; this will disturb them and render them less troublesome. As soon as the tops are two inches high, run a corn-plow five inches deep *close* to the hills, turning the furrows *from* the rows.

Plow both ways twice between the rows, finishing on the rows running east and west, which will give the sun's rays a better chance to warm the ground properly. Standing on the squares of earth, warmed on all sides by the air and sunlight, the potatoes will grow amazingly. Just as soon as the tops have attained a height of six or seven inches, hitch a strong horse to a two-horse plow, and turn furrows fully seven inches deep midway between the rows *to* the hills. Plow

twice between the rows both ways; and if the ground be a side-hill, turn the first furrow between the rows up-hill, which will leave the rows in better shape. Hoeing is often wholly unnecessary; but where, from weeds or poor plowing, it is needed, draw mellow earth to the plants with the hoe, keeping the top of the hills somewhat hollow to catch the rains. Then, so far as stirring the soil is concerned, *let it alone.*

After potatoes are fairly up, their cultivation should be crowded through with all possible speed, or at least as rapidly as the growth of the tops will permit.

If the last plowing be deferred until the vines are large, a large proportion of small potatoes is sure to be the consequence. After a certain stage of growth, new tubers are formed each time the soil is disturbed; these never fully develop, they rob those first formed, and make the crop much inferior to what it should be. By the mode of culture described, the ground is made warm and mellow close up to the seed-potatoes, the roots soon fill the whole hill, and tubers are formed that have nothing to do but to grow. The writer is aware flat culture has strong advocates; but, after many experiments, he is convinced that hills are much the best.

PLASTER.

However much lime or other fertilizers may be applied to the soil, still great benefit is derived from the use of plaster, (sulphate of lime.)

After all, plaster is the main dependence of the potato-grower, a help on which he may rely with the utmost confidence. Astonishing results are obtained from its use, when applied in a proper manner. The writer has seen a field, all of the same soil, all prepared alike, and all planted with the same variety at the same time, on one half of which, that had no plaster, the yield was but sixty bushels per acre, and many rotten; the other part, to which plaster was applied in the manner hereafter explained, yielded three hundred and sixty bushels per acre, and not an unsound one among them.

The action of plaster is often puzzling. From the fact that where land has been strongly limed, a small quantity of plaster applied shows such decided benefit, there would seem plausibility in Liebig's theory that its effects must be traceable not to the lime, but to the sulphuric acid. The ammonia in rain-water in the form of carbonate (a volatile salt) is decomposed by plaster, the sulphuric acid having greater affinity for it, thus forming two new compounds, sulphate of ammonia and carbonate of lime. But as arable soil has the same property of absorbing ammonia from the air and rain-water, and fixing it in the same or even a higher degree than lime, there is only the sulphuric acid left to look to for an explanation of the favorable action of plaster on the growth of plants.

It is found that plaster in contact with soil undergoes decomposition, part of the lime separating from the sulphuric acid, and magnesia and potash taking its place, quite contrary to the ordinary affinities.

These facts show that the action of plaster is very complex, and that it promotes the distribution of both magnesia and potash in the ground, exercising a chemical action upon the soil which extends to any depth of it; and that, in consequence of the chemical and mechanical modifications of the earth, particles of certain nutritive elements become accessible and available to plants that were not so before.

It is said plaster is of most bene-

fit in wet seasons; such is not always the case. It is certainly beneficial to clover, wet or dry; so of potatoes.

A few years since, when the drought was so intense in this section as to render the general potato crop almost a total failure, the writer produced a plentiful crop by the use of plaster alone. On examination at the dryest time, the bottoms of the hills were found to be literally dust, yet in this dust the tubers were swelling finely: the leaves and vines were of a deep rich green, and remained so until frost, while other fields in sight, planted with the same variety, but not treated with plaster, were brown, dead, and not worth digging. That gypsum attracts moisture may be proved by plastering a hill of corn and leaving a hill by it unplastered; the dew will be found deposited in greater abundance on the plastered hill. But, according to Liebig, certain products of the chemical action of plaster enter into and are incorporated with the structure of the plant, closing its breathing pores to such an extent that the plant is enabled to withstand a drought which would prove fatal to it unassisted.

Certain it is that plaster renders plants less palatable to insects, and, so far as the writer's experiments extend, it is fatal to many of the fungi family. To obtain the best results, the vines of potatoes should be dusted with plaster as soon as they are fairly through the soil, again immediately after the last plowing and hoeing, and, for reasons hereafter given, at intervals throughout the whole growing season. The first application may be light, the second heavier, and thereafter it should be bountifully applied, say two hundred pounds per acre at one sowing.

THE POTATO-ROT—ITS CAUSE

The year 1845 will ever be memo

rable by its giving birth to a disease which threatened the entire destruction of the potato crop, and which caused suffering and pecuniary ruin to an incredible extent throughout Europe.

The potato, at the time of the appearance of the potato disease, was almost the sole dependence of the common people of Ireland for food. That over-populated country experienced more actual suffering in consequence of the potato disease than has any other from the same cause. Although this disease has never, in this country, prevailed to the same ruinous extent that it has in some others, yet we are yearly reminded of its existence, and in some seasons and localities its destructive effects are seriously apparent.

The final or culminating cause of the disease known as the "potato-rot" is *Botrytis (peronospora) infestans.* This may be induced by many and various predisposing causes, such as feebleness of constitution of the variety planted, rendering them an easy prey to the disease; by planting on low, moist land, or on land highly enriched by nitrogenous manures, causing a morbid growth which invites the disease; also by insects or their larvæ puncturing or eating off the leaves or vines. But by far the most wide-spread and most common cause of the disease is sudden changes of atmospheric temperature, particularly when accompanied by rain. Drought, though quite protracted and severe, unless accompanied by strong drying winds, and followed by sudden and great reduction of temperature, seldom affects the potato seriously. It is not uncommon in the Northern States, during the months of August and September, for strong westerly winds to prevail for many days in succession. These winds, coming from the great American desert, are almost wholly devoid of moisture, and their aridity is often such that vegetation withers before them as at the touch of fire. Evaporation is increased in a prodigiously rapid ratio with the velocity of wind. The effects of the excessive exhalation from the leaves of plants exposed to the sweep of such drying winds are at once seriously apparent.

When these winds finally cease, the atmosphere has a low relative humidity, not enough moisture remains in the air to prevent radiation; the heat absorbed by the earth through the day is, during the bright, cloudless night, rapidly radiated and lost in space, and a reduction in temperature of twenty to thirty degrees is the consequence.

In the first place, the potato-vines suffer by excessive exhalation; in the second, by sudden reduction of temperature, and, though not frozen, their functions are much deranged, and their vitality greatly enfeebled. To use a common expression, the plant "has caught a violent cold that has settled on the lungs."

The leaves (which are the lungs of plants) now fail to perform their functions properly. The points of many of the leaves turn brown, curl up, and die.

The ascending sap, not being fully elaborated by the diseased leaves, oozes out through the skin of the stalk in a thick, viscous state, and the plant to all appearance is in a state of consumption.

At this stage the ever-present minute spores of the *Botrytis infestans* eagerly pounce on the sickly plant, fastening themselves on its most diseased parts. The *Botrytis infestans* is a cryptogamous plant, and is included in the Mucidineous family, (moulds.) It is a vegetable parasite preying upon the living potato plant, like lice or other animal parasites upon the animal species.

At first this mould forms webby, creeping filaments, known in botanical language as mycelium. These root-like fibres then branch out, sending out straight or decumbent articulated stems. These bead-like joints fill up successively with seeds or spores, which are discharged at the proper time to multiply the species.

Under favorable conditions of warmth and moisture, the mycelium spreads very rapidly. Spores are soon formed and matured, to be carried to plants not yet infected. Rains also wash the seminal dust down the plant, causing it to fasten and grow on the vine near the ground. The roots of the parasite penetrate and split up the stalk even to the medullary canal.

These roots exude a poisonous substance, which is carried by the elaborated descending sap down to the tubers, and as the largest tubers require the largest amount of elaborated sap for their development, they will, consequently, receive the greatest quantity of the vitiating principle, and will, on digging, be found a mass of rottenness, when the smaller ones are often but slightly affected. The *Botrytis infestans* can not gain a lodgment on vines that are truly healthy and vigorous, high authority to the contrary notwithstanding.

Healthy varieties, growing in a sheltered situation on dry, new soil, to which no nitrogenous manures have been applied, can not be infected, though brushed with other vines covered with the fungus. Different varieties, and sometimes different members of the same variety, are not always alike affected by the disease, though growing in the same hill.

As will be noticed, the potato disease is rather an effect than a cause, and appears to have been designed to prevent members enfeebled by accident or otherwise from propagating their species by putting such members out of existence. Ozone, supposed to be a peculiar form of oxygen, is exhaled from every part of the green surface of plants in health, and effectually repels the attacks of mildew; but it is found that when the atmosphere is very dry, or, on the other hand, very humid, plants cease to evolve ozone, and are therefore unprotected. Winds from the ocean are strongly ozonic, and it is ascertained that plants growing on soil to which salt has been applied evolve more ozone than others. Hence the benefit derived from the use of salt on potato lands.

The "Black knot," another species of fungus that attacks the branches of the plum and Morello cherry, operates very similarly to the potato mildew. The roots of the parasite penetrate and split up the cellular tissue of the branch on which it fastens, and if the limb be not promptly amputated, the descending sap carries the deleterious principle through the whole system, and the following year the disease appears in a greatly aggravated form in every part of the whole tree. The remedy in this case is prompt amputation of the part diseased on its first appearance, and a judicious application of salt to the soil.

Common salt, to a certain extent, is as beneficial to some plants as to animals; and every intelligent farmer knows that if salt be withheld from the bovine *genus* for any considerable length of time, the general health droops and parasites are sure to abound. The object of nature in bringing into existence the large family of mildews, each member of which is a perfect plant in its way, and as capable of performing its functions as the oak of the forest, was undoubtedly to prevent propagation from sickly stock, and by the decomposition of feeble plants to make room and enrich the soil for the better development of healthier plants. But it by no means follows that, because a plant is attacked by mildew, it must necessarily be left to die, any more than it follows that, because an animal is infested with vermin, it should be let alone to be eaten up by them.

REMEDY FOR THE POTATO-ROT.

In treating for the potato-rot, "an ounce of prevention is worth a pound of cure;" for when leaves or vines are once dead, they ever remain so. All that can be done for potatoes infested is to stop the mildew from spreading, by destroying it where it is, and by strengthening "those things which remain." The writer was led to the adoption of the remedy proposed by experiments made upon fruits.

Every one who has an apple or pear-orchard must have observed that mildew of fruit supervenes after some sudden change of temperature, especially when accompanied by rain. Spots of mildew invariably form on the young fruit immediately after a cold night, when the thermometer has indicated a change of twenty to twenty-five degrees. This growth of mildew takes place when the apples are of various sizes, from the earliest formation to the size of large marbles. These fungous growths appear as dark-colored spots, which arrest the growth of the apple immediately beneath, causing it to become distorted, while the expansion and contraction bring on diseased action, which results in the cracking and general scabbiness of the fruit.

Knowing that dry-rot (*Merulius Lachrymans*, (Schum,) another species of fungus, was remedied by an application of sulphuric acid, I thought it might possibly destroy the fruit mildew. An application of plaster, (gypsum,) which is composed of lime and sulphuric acid, was made with the happiest results. It was found that an apple dusted with ground plaster at its first formation remained free from mildew and came to maturity, while apples growing by it, but not so treated, became scabby and worthless. It was also ascertained that a thorough application of plaster destroyed the mildew after it had formed, and that such fruit came to maturity. On the potato mildew, so far as the writer's experience extends, plaster, if applied early, is a perfect prevention, and if not delayed too long after the disease appears, is a certain remedy.

The vines should be watched closely, and on the first appearance of the disease plaster should be applied; not merely sowing it broadcast, but dashing it over and under the vines, bringing it in contact with the stalks, using a handful to three or four hills. Plaster for this purpose should be very dry and powdery, and should be applied when the air is still. One application is seldom sufficient; it should be renewed as often as circumstances require. Examine the vines about three days after a cold night, or about the same length of time after a heavy rain. If the leaves begin to curl and wither, apply plaster at once; and, in short, whenever the vines show any signs of drooping, be the cause bites of insects, excessive aridity, or excessive humidity of the atmosphere, or sudden change of temperature, drooping from any cause whatever indicates the approach of mildew, which should be promptly met with an application of plaster. As before stated, plaster the vines as soon as they are up, again after the last plowing and hoeing; after that, one, two, or three times, as circumstances indicate.

By this method the vines are kept of a bright lively green, and the tubers are kept swelling until growth is stopped by frost. Another point gained is, potatoes so grown are so sound and free from disease as to be easily kept for spring market without loss by rot.

Whether the surprising effects of plaster on the potato mildew is attributable to the sulphuric acid, to the lime, or to its simply being a dust, has not been determined. It is well known that the fruits of a vineyard or orchard in close proximity to a dusty and much frequented highway are remarkably free from mildew, which can only be due to dust settling on the trees and fruit. But in the case of plaster, the writer is inclined to believe its efficacy is mainly due to the sulphuric acid, probably assisted by the lime in a state of dust. Be this as it may, it matters not. The result is all that can be desired; the remedy is easily applied, costs but a trifle, and a single season's trial is all that is needed to convince the most skeptical grower of its merits.

DIGGING AND STORING

Is full half the labor of growing and securing a crop of potatoes. Digging is a long, laborious task. Many small fortunes are sunk yearly by inventors in experimenting with and constructing "potato-diggers;" but, so far, no machine has done the work properly except under the most favorable circumstances. Stones, vines, and weeds are obstacles not yet fully overcome. Many tubers are left covered with earth, and so lost; and besides, some machines so bruise the tubers in digging as to injure their appearance and keeping qualities. Undoubtedly, the day will come when the great bulk of potatoes will be dug well and rapidly by horse-power; but until that day does come, the potato-hook must be used.

Much of the back-ache and general unpleasantness incident to digging is avoided, or greatly mitigated, by having the potatoes large and sound, turning out a peck to the hill, especially if the digger is the owner of the crop.

Digging should be done only when the ground is dry, that the potatoes may come out clean and bright. A small plow, to turn a light furrow from each side of the rows, is some help. Pull up the vines, and lay them down so that they will be covered by the dirt dug from the hill. Commence on one side of the hill; press the hook or hoe down, so that it will reach a trifle below the potatoes, and draw the implement firmly toward you. Repeat the operation, each time placing the tool a few inches further in or across the hill, until the whole hill is dug. By this method the potatoes will not be bruised; whereas, if the digging be commenced in the centre of the hill, many potatoes will be sacrificed and much injured. Potatoes should be picked up as soon and as fast as dug; and immediately covered with straw or other material, to protect them from the light. A few hours' strong sunshine will ruin the best potato ever grown. Light changes the natural color to green, and renders the potato so bitter and unpalatable as to be wholly unfit to eat.

Owing to the inconsiderate way in which potatoes are often dug, and the light to which they are exposed while being transported to and while in market, the denizens of our cities seldom, if ever, taste this vegetable in its greatest excellence. If to be stored in the cellar, the potatoes should be left in the field, in heaps covered with straw, until the sweating is over, and then be removed to the cellar and lightly covered with dry sand, or earth, just sufficient to exclude the light.

If to be buried in the field, choose a dry, sideling place; scrape out a slight hollow, by merely removing the surface soil with a hoe; into this, pile

ten to twelve bushels; place the potatoes properly, and cover them carefully with clean straw, six inches
deep; cover over the straw with four
or five inches of earth, except a small
opening at the top; over this opening
place a board or flat stone, elevated a
little on one side, to lead off the rain.

Let them remain so until the sweating is completely over, or so long as
prudence will permit; and when cold
weather fairly sets in, add more earth
to keep from freezing, leaving only a
wisp of straw protruding through to
carry off any foul air that may be
generated.

Where the winters are intensely
cold, it is best to cover but lightly
with earth, say five or six inches deep;
and when freezing is becoming severe, spread over the heap buckwheat
straw, or coarse manure, to the depth
of six inches. There is danger in
covering very deep at first, especially
if the autumn should prove warm.
If kept too warm, rot is sure to ensue.
Experience shows that any vegetable
keeps better buried in pits that contain not more than ten or twelve
bushels each.

Where large quantities are to be
buried, it is advisable to open a long,
shallow, broad trench, leading up and
down a hill, if possible, to secure good
drainage. Commence, at either end,
by placing a desirable quantity of
potatoes as soon as dug; next to
these put a little straw; against the
straw place about six inches of earth;
then more straw and more potatoes;
and so keep on until the trench is full.
A few furrows plowed on each side
assist in covering; and make a drain
to lead off the rains, which is a matter of the first importance. By this
method each lot of potatoes is kept
separate; and any section can be
opened at any time to be taken to
market, without endangering the
others.

Potatoes buried properly are usually
of better flavor in the spring than it is
possible for potatoes to be which are
kept in a common cellar.

And here let me add that, if leaves
from the woods be used instead of
straw, to cover potatoes to be buried,
such potatoes will be of better flavor;
and further, if nothing but dry earth
comes in contact with them, they will
be better still. Straw is used for the
twofold purpose of securing an air-
chamber to keep out frost, and to
prevent the earth from mingling with
the tubers on opening the pits.

INSECTS INJURIOUS TO THE PO-TATO.

There are ten distinct species of
insects preying upon the potato-plant
within the limits of the United States.
Many of these ten species are confined within certain geographical limits. Their habits and history differ
very widely. Some attack the potato
both in the larva state and in the perfect or winged state; others in the
perfect or winged state alone; and
others again in the larva state alone.

In the case of seven of these insects, there is but one single brood
every year; while of the remaining
three there are every year from two
to three broods, each of them generated by females belonging to preceding broods. Eight of the ten feed
externally on the leaves and tender
stems of the potato; while two of
them burrow, like a borer, exclusively
in the larger stalks.

Each of these ten species has its
peculiar insect enemies; and a mode
of attack which will prove very successful against some of them will
often turn out to be worthless when
employed against the remainder.

The Stalk-Borer, * (*Gortyna ni-
tela*, Guenee.)—This larva (Fig. 2,)

* Where no hair-lines are given, the insects are
represented life-size.

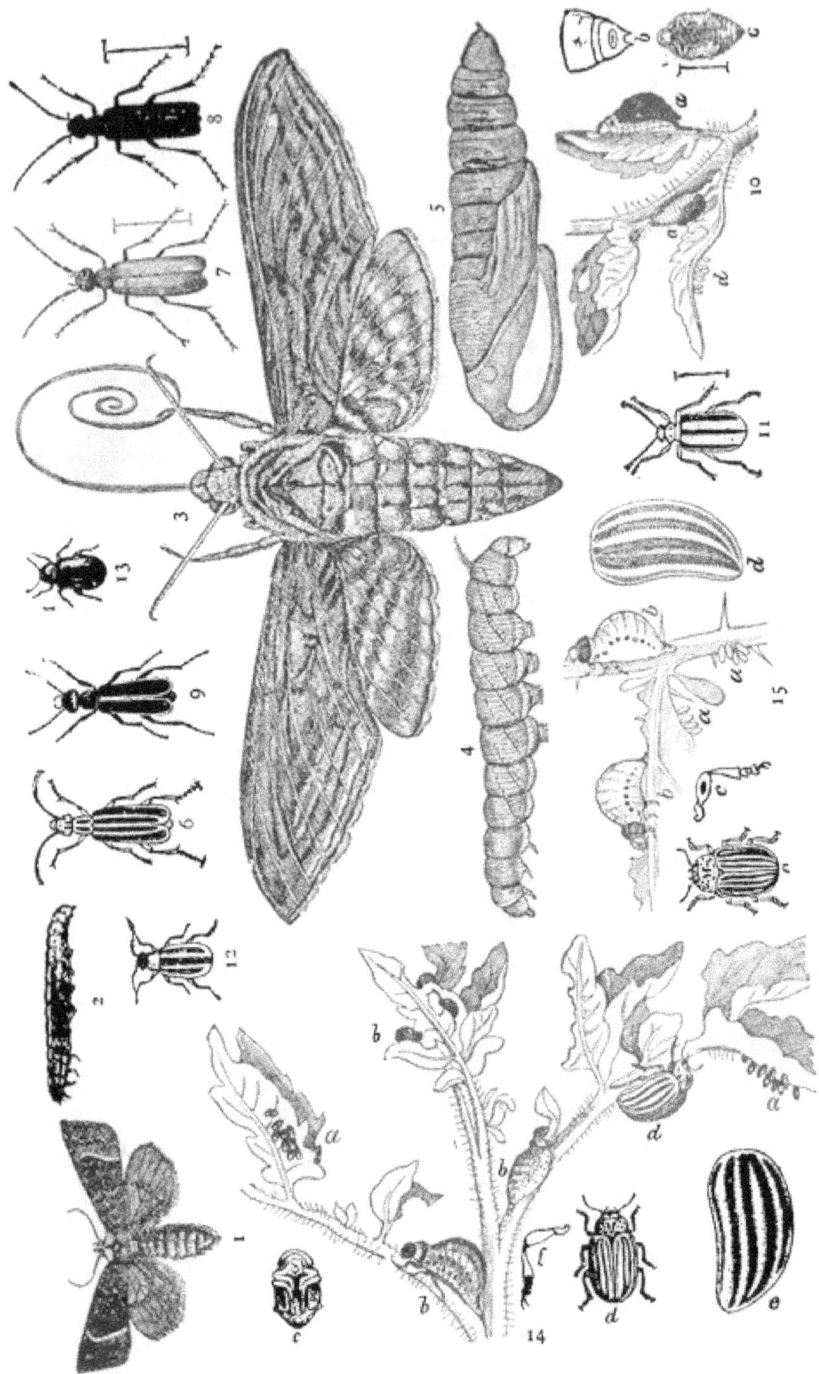

commonly burrows in the large stalks of the potato. It occurs also in the stalks of the tomato, in those of the dahlia and aster, and other garden flowers. It is sometimes found boring through the cob of growing Indian corn. It is particularly partial to the stem of the common cocklebur, (*Zanthium strumarium ;*) and if it would only confine itself to such noxious weeds, it might be considered more of a friend than an enemy. It is yearly becoming more numerous and more destructive. It is found over a great extent of country ; and is particularly numerous in the valley of the Mississippi north of the Ohio River. The larva of the stalk-borer moth leaves the stalk in which it burrowed about the latter part of July, and descends a little below the surface of the earth, where in about three days it changes into the pupa, or chrysalis state.

The winged insect (Fig. 1,) which belongs to the same extensive group of moths (*Noctua* family, or owlet moths) to which all the cut-worm moths appertain, emerges from under ground from the end of August to the middle of September. Hence it is evident that some few, at all events, of the female moths must live through the winter, in obscure places, to lay eggs upon the plants they infest the following spring : for otherwise, as there is no young potato, or other plants, for them to lay eggs upon in the autumn, the whole breed would die out in a single year. This insect, in sections where it is numerous, does more injury to the potato crop than is generally supposed.

The Potato-Stalk Weevil, (*Baridius trinotatus.* Say.)—This insect is more particularly a southern species, occurring abundantly in the Middle States, and in the southern parts of Missouri, Illinois, and Indiana. It appears to be totally unknown in New-England.

The female of this beetle deposits a single egg in an oblong slit, about one eighth of an inch long, which it has previously formed with its beak in the stalk of the potato. The larva subsequently hatches out, and bores into the heart of the stalk, alway proceeding downward toward the root. When full grown, it is a little more than one fourth of an inch in length, and is a soft, whitish, legless grub, with a scaly head. Hence it can always be readily distinguished from the larva of the stalk-borer, which has invariably sixteen legs, no matter how small it may be. Unlike this last insect, it becomes a pupa in the interior of the potato-stalk which it inhabits : and it comes out in the beetle state about the last of August or beginning of September.

The stalk inhabited by the larva wilts and dies. The perfect beetle, like many other snout-beetles, must of course live through the winter, to reproduce its species the following spring. In Southern Pennsylvania, some years, nearly every stalk of extensive fields is infested by this insect, causing the premature decay of the vines, and giving them the appearance of having been scalded. In some districts of Illinois, the potato crop has, in some seasons, been utterly ruined by this snout-beetle, many vines having a dozen larvæ in them. This insect attacks no plant but the potato.

The Potato-Worm, (*Sphinx* 5-*maculata,* Haworth.)—This well-known insect, the larva of which (Fig. 3.) is usually called the potato-worm, is more common on the closely allied tomato. the leaves of which it often clears off very completely in particular spots in a single night. When full-fed, which is usually about the last of August, the potato-worm burrows under the ground, and shortly afterward transforms into the pupa state, (Fig. 5.) The pupa is often dug up in the spring from the ground where tomatoes or potatoes were grown in the preceding season, and most persons that meet with it suppose that the singular jug-handled appendage at one end of it is its *tail.* In reality, however, it is the *tongue-case*, and contains the long, pliable tongue which the future moth will employ in lapping the nectar of flowers. The moth itself (Fig. 4) was formerly confounded with the tobacco-worm moth, (*Sphinx Carolina*, Linnæus,) which it very closely resembles, having the same series of orange-colored spots on each side of the abdomen.

The gray and black markings, however, of the wings differ perceptibly in the two species; and in the tobacco-worm moth there is always a more or less faint white spot, or a dot, near the centre of the front wing, which is never met with in the other species. The potato-worm often feeds on the leaves of the tobacco plant in the Northern States. In the Southern States, in Mexico and the West-Indies, the true potato-worm is unknown, and it is the tobacco-worm that the tobacco-grower has to fight. The potato-worm, however, is never known to injure the potato crop to any serious extent.

The Striped Blister-Beetle,

(*Lytta vittata*, Fabr.) This insect (Fig. 6) is almost exclusively a southern species, occurring in some years very abundantly on the potato-vines in Southern Illinois, and also in Missouri, and according to Dr. Harris, it is occasionally found even in New-England. In some specimens the broad outer black stripe on the wing-cases is divided lengthwise by a slen-

der yellow line, so that, instead of *two*, there are *three* black stripes on each wing-case; and often in the same field may be noticed all the intermediate grades; thus proving that the four-striped individuals do not form a distinct species, as was supposed by the European entomologist Fabricius, but are mere varieties of the same species to which the sixth-striped individual appertains.

The striped blister-beetle lives under ground and feeds upon various roots during the larva state, and emerges to attack the foliage of the potato only when it has passed into the perfect or beetle state.

This insect, in common with our other blister-beetles, has the same properties as the imported Spanish fly, and any of them will raise just as good a blister as that does, and are equally poisonous when taken internally in large doses. Where the striped blister-beetle is numerous, it is a great pest and very destructive to the potato crop. It eats the leaves so full of holes that the plant finally dies from loss of sap and the want of sufficient leaves to elaborate its juices. In some places they are driven off the plants (with bushes) on a pile of hay or straw, and burned. Some have been successful in ridding their fields of them by placing straw or hay between the rows of potatoes, and then setting it on fire. The insects, it is said, by this means are nearly all destroyed, and the straw burning very quickly, does not injure the vines.

The Ash-Gray Blister-Beetle, (*Lytta cinera*, Fabr.)—This species (Fig. 7. male) is the one commonly found in the more northerly parts of the Northern States, where it usually takes the place of the striped blister-beetle before mentioned. It is of a uniform ash-gray color. It attacks not only the potato-vines but

also the honey locusts, and especially the Windsor bean. In particular years it has been known, in conjunction with the rose-bug, *(Macrodactylus subspinosus,* Linn.,) to swarm upon every apple-tree in some orchards in Illinois, not only eating the foliage, but gnawing into the young apples.

This beetle does considerable damage to the potato crop, especially in the North-Western States. Like the other members of the *(Lytta)* family, it lives under ground while in the lava state, and is troublesome only when in the perfect or winged state.

The Black-Rat Blister-Beetle, *(Lytta murina,* Le Conte.)

—This species (Fig. 8,) is entirely black. There is a very similar species, the black blister-beetle, (*Lytta atrata,* Fabr.,)from which the black-rat blister-beetle is distinguishable only by having four raised lines placed lengthwise upon each wing-case, and by the two first joints of the antennæ being greatly dilated and lengthened in the males, of the lath species. It is asserted by some authors that the black blister-beetle is injurious to the potato; but I can not see how it could do much damage to that crop, as the perfect insect does not appear until late in August, when the potato crop is nearly out of its reach. Not so, however, with the black-rat blister-beetle, which is on hand ready for business early in the season. This insect does considerable damage to the potato in Iowa, and neighboring States; it is also found, though in not so great numbers, throughout the whole of the Northern States.

The Margined Blister-Beetle, *(Lytta marginata,* Fabr.)

—This species (Fig. 9) may be at once recognized by its general black color, and the ash-gray edging to its wing-cases. It usually feeds on certain wild plants, but does not object to a diet of potato-leaves. Though found over a large extent of country, it seldom appears in numbers large enough to damage the potato crop materially. Like other blister-beetles, it goes under ground to pass into the pupa state, and attacks the potato only when it is in the perfect or winged state.

The Three-Lined Leaf-Beetle, *(Lema trilineata,* Olivier.)

The larva of the three-lined leaf-beetle may be distinguished from all other insects which prey upon the potato by its habit of covering itself with its own excrement. In Figure 10, *a,* this larva is shown in profile, both full and half grown, covered with the soft, greenish excrementitious matter which from time to time it discharges. Figure 10, *c,* gives a somewhat magnified view of the pupa, and Figure 10, *b,* shows the last few joints of the abdomen of the larva, magnified and viewed from above. The vent of the larva, as will be seen from this last figure, is situated on the upper surface of the last joint, so that its excrement naturally falls upon its back, and by successive discharges is crowded forward toward its head, till the whole upper surface is covered with it. There are several other larva, feeding upon other plants, which wear cloaks of this strange material.

Many authors suppose that the object of the larva in all these cases is to protect itself from the heat of the sun. In all probability the real aim of nature in the case of all these larvæ is to defend them from the attacks of birds and of cannibal and parasitic insects.

There are two broods of this insect every year. The first brood of larvæ may be found on the potato-vine toward the latter end of June, and the second in August.

The first brood stays under ground

about a fortnight before it emerges in the perfect beetle state, and the second brood stays under ground all winter, and only emerges at the beginning of the following June.

The perfect beetle (Fig. 11) is of a pale yellow color, with three black stripes on its back, and bears a strong resemblance to the cucumber-bug, (*Diabrotica vittata*, Fabr. Fig. 12.)

From this last species, however, it may be distinguished by its somewhat larger size, and by the remarkable pinching-in of the thorax, so as to make quite a lady-like waist there, or what naturalists call a " constriction." The female, after coupling, lays her yellow eggs (Fig. 10, *d*) on the under surface of the leaves of the potato plant. The larvæ hatching, when full grown descend into the ground, where they transform to pupæ (Fig. 10, *c*) within a small oval chamber, from which in time the perfect beetle emerges.

This insect in certain seasons is a great pest in the Eastern and Middle States, but has never yet occurred in the Mississippi Valley in such numbers as to be materially injurious.

The Cucumber Flea-Beetle,

(*Haltica cucumeris*, Harris.) This nimble minute beetle (Fig. 13) belongs to the flea-beetles, (*Haltica* family,) the same sub-group of the leaf-beetles (*Phytophaga*) to which also appertains the notorious steel-blue flea-beetle (*Haltica chalybea*, Illiger) that is such a pest to the vineyardist. Like all the rest of the flea-beetles, it has its hind thighs greatly enlarged, which enables it to jump with much agility. It is not peculiar to the potato, but infests a great variety of plants, including the cucumber, from which it derives its name. It eats minute round holes in the leaf of the plant it infests, but does not always penetrate entirely through it.

The larva feeds internally upon the substance of the leaf, and goes under ground to assume the pupa state. It passes through all its stages in about a month, and there are two or three broods of them in the course of the same season. This is emphatically the greatest insect pest that the potato-grower has to contend with in Pennsylvania. It abounds throughout most of the Northern, Middle, and Western States. Large fields of potatoes can any summer be seen in the Middle States much injured by this minute insect, every leaf apparently completely riddled with minute round holes, and the stalks and leaves appearing yellow and seared. Plaster frequently and bountifully applied is sure to prevent the attacks of this insect, or to disperse it after it has commenced operations.

The Colorado Potato-Bug,

(*Doryphora* 10—*lineata*, Say.)—This insect, which, according to Dr. Walsh, has in the North-West alone damaged the potato crop to the amount of one million seven hundred and fifty thousand dollars, came originally from the Rocky Mountains, where it was found forty-five years ago, feeding on a wild species of potato peculiar to that region, (*Solanum rostratum*, Dunal.) When civilization marched up the Rocky Mountains, and potatoes began to be grown in that region, this highly improved pest acquired the habit of feeding upon the cultivated potato. It went from potato-patch to potato-patch, moving eastward at the rate of about sixty miles a year, and is now firmly established over all the country extending from Indiana to its old feeding-grounds in the Rocky Mountains. In about twelve years it will have reached the Atlantic coast.

There is another very closely allied species, known as the Bogus Colorado

potato-bug, (*coryphora juncta*, Ger-
mor,) which has existed throughout
a great part of the United States from
time immemorial. This latter insect,
however, feeds almost exclusively on
the horse-nettle, (*Solanum carolinense*,
Linn.,) and is never known to injure
the potato. Both insects are figured,
so that one need not be mistaken for
the other.

Figure 14, *b, b, b,* gives a view of
the larva of the true Colorado potato-
bug, in various positions and stages
of its existence. Figure 15, *b, b,* of
that of the bogus Colorado potato-
bug. It will be seen at once that the
head of the former is black, and the
first joint behind the head is pale and
edged with black behind only; that
there is a double row of black spots
along the side of the body; and that
the legs are black. In the other larva,
(Fig. 15, *b,*) on the contrary, the
head is of a pale color, the first joint
behind the head is tinged with dusk
and edged all round with black; there
is but a single row of spots along the
side of the body, and the legs are
pale.

Figure 14, *d, d,* exhibits the true
Colorado potato-bug; Figure 15, the
bogus Colorado potato-bug; each of
its natural size. Figure 14, *e,* shows
the *left* wing-case enlarged, and Figure 15, *e,* an enlarged leg of the latter.
On a close inspection, it will be per-
ceived that in the former (Fig. 14,
e) the boundary of each dark stripe
on the wing-cases toward the middle
is studded with confused and irregu-
lar punctures, partly inside and partly outside the edge of the dark stripe;
that it is the third and fourth dark
stripes, counting from the outside, that
are united behind, and that both the
knees and feet are black.

In Figure 15, *d,* on the contrary, it
is the second and third stripes—not
the third and fourth—counting from
the outside, that are united behind,

and the leg is entirely pale, except
a black spot on the middle of the
front of the thigh. The eggs (Fig.
14, *a, a,* and Fig. 15, *d, d*) are yellow, and are always laid on the under
side of the leaf in patches of from
twenty to thirty; those of the bogus
are of a lighter color. Each female
of the true Colorado potato-bug lays,
according to Dr. Schirmer, about seven hundred eggs. In about six days
the eggs hatch into larvæ, which feed
on the foliage of the potato plant
about seventeen days; they then
descend to the ground, where they
change into pupæ at the surface of
the earth. The perfect beetle appears about ten to fourteen days after
the pupa is formed, begins to pair in
about seven days, and on the four-
teenth day begins to deposit her eggs.
There are three broods of this insect
every year. Neither geese, ducks,
turkeys, nor barn-yard fowl will touch
the larva of the Colorado potato-bug
when it is offered to them, and there
are numerous authentic cases on re-
cord where persons who have scalded to death quantities of these larvæ,
and inhaled the fumes of their bodies,
have been taken seriously ill, and even
been confined to their beds for many
days in consequence. It is also re-
ported to have produced poisonous
effects on several persons who han-
dled them incautiously with naked
hands. Various plans have been
tried to destroy this persistent enemy
of the potato plant. Powdered hellebore is said to have been used with
effect as a means of destroying the
pest. It should be dusted on and
under the foliage when the plant is
wet with dew. Hellebore, however,
is a dangerous remedy on account of
its poisonous qualities. A mixture
of one part salt, ten parts soap, and
twenty parts water, applied to every
part of the plants with a syringe, is
quite effectual. Several cannibal and

one parasitic insect are known to prey upon the larva of the Colorado potato-bug, and the eggs in vast numbers are eaten by several species of ladybirds and their larva.

GENERAL REMARKS ON INSECTS.

The time is not far distant when the American farmer will be obliged to put forth greater efforts to destroy noxious insects than he has hitherto. It is a well-known fact that noxious insects are increasing in a rapid rate throughout every part of our land. The country is becoming so " buggy " that eternal vigilance is the price of every thing produced from the soil.

Close observers calculate that more fruits of various kinds and varieties are annually destroyed or rendered worthless by insects than are gathered and used by man. The cotton-worm, the wheat-midge, the canker-worms, the potato-bugs, are each every year increasing in numbers and destructiveness.

The "curculio" alone destroys millions of dollars' worth of fruit annually.

It is a safe estimate, all things considered, that, if noxious insects of all descriptions could at once be annihilated throughout our country, and mildews of various classes be effectually held in check, the cost of living to our people would, in a short time, be reduced to one third of its present amount. It is disheartening to see what a vast amount of grains, fruits, and vegetables is annually eaten up by the larvæ, or appropriated by the perfect insects of various classes, merely for the sake of propagating their abominable species. Yet, in view of all the devastation, but feeble effort is made to abate the evil. Birds, many species of which nature seemingly designed on purpose to keep insects in check, are wantonly shot by lazy boys and indolent men, who range the fields and forests, killing all, from the humming-bird to the crow. Legislative enactments made expressly to protect the insectivorous songsters are every day violated with impunity. One man plants an orchard and does all he can to destroy noxious insects; another man near him also has an orchard, but his orchard serves no purpose but to propagate "curculios," "canker-worms," "barklice," "tent caterpillars," "codling moths," etc., for his neighbors, and, as a matter of course, the whole neighborhood swarms with noxious insects. If all cultivators would act in concert and with a will, insects might be reduced in numbers very rapidly. Most moths of night-flying insects are attracted to and destroyed by small bonfires kindled in still evenings during the summer months.

Bottles half-filled with sweetened water, hung here and there, will trap countless bugs. Strong soap-suds applied immediately after they hatch is a sure remedy for plant lice. Molasses and water, to which a little arsenic has been added, placed in shallow dishes among the vines, is good medicine for potato-bugs, and all bugs in general. A lighted lamp placed in the centre of a common milk-pan, partly filled with water, the whole elevated a few feet from the ground, will, on a still evening, attract and destroy the wheat-midge and similar insects in great numbers. The calculations of the "curculio" and "codling moth" are brought to naught by turning hogs into the orchard to eat the stung fruit as it falls, and the larva that depastures upon the leaves of the current and gooseberry is destroyed by syringing the plants with a mixture of soap, salt, and water.

VALUE OF THE POTATO AS CATTLE FOOD.

The constituents of the potato are.

according to different authorities, as follows:

Water............75.2	Or economically :
Casein 1.4	Water................75.2
Starch... ....15.5	Flesh-formers........1.4
Dextrine 0.4	Fat-formers..........18.9
Sugar 3.2	Accessories..........3.6
Fat 0.2	Mineral matter.......0.9
Fibre 3.2	
Mineral matter......0.9	

Of the high value of potatoes, when used in connection with other food, there is not a shadow of doubt. All experimenters and observers in the economy of food agree in saying that they are of the highest utility; but they must be used with other food whose constituents are different from those of the root.

The analysis shows that potatoes surpass in the fat-producing principles the nutritious or flesh-forming in such proportions that they could not alone sustain the composition of the blood; for an animal fed alone on these tubers would be obliged to consume such quantities to provide the blood with the requisite proportion of albumen that, even if the process of digestion were not discontinued, there would be a superabundance of fat accumulated beyond the power of the oxygen to consume, which would successively absorb from the albuminous substance a part of its vital elements, and thus a check would be caused in the endless change of matter in the tissues in the nutritive and regressive transformations.

Potatoes, then, to be of most value as food for cattle, should be fed in connection with grain, or with other roots in which the flesh-forming element predominates. There seems to be no doubt that the tubers are of most value when cooked, although some authors affirm to the contrary. It seems possible to prove this on philosophical principles; for it is well known that the starch contained in the potato is incapable of affording nourishment until the containing globules are broken, and one of the most efficient means of doing this seems to be by heat.

Boussingault, in speaking of the economy of cooking potatoes, says, "The potato is frequently steamed or boiled first; yet I can say positively that horned cattle do extremely well upon raw potatoes, and at Bechelbrunn our cows never have them otherwise than raw. They are never boiled, save for horses and hogs. The best mode of dealing with them is to steam them; they need never be so thoroughly boiled as when they are to serve for the food of man. The steamed or boiled potatoes are crushed between two rollers, or simply broken with a wooden spade, and mixed with cut hay or straw or chaff, before being served out. It may not be unnecessary to observe that by steaming potatoes lose no weight; hence we conclude that the nutritive equivalent for the boiled is the same as that of the raw tuber.

"Nevertheless, it is possible that the amylaceous principle is rendered more easily assimilable by boiling, and that by this means the tubers actually become more nutritious. Some have proposed to roast potatoes in the oven, and there can be little question that heated in this way they answer admirably for fattening hogs, and even oxen. Done in the oven, potatoes may be brought to a state in which they may perfectly supply the place of corn in feeding horses and other cattle."

The apparent contradiction in the remarks will be observed; but the evident leaning in favor of cooked potatoes shows that Boussingault, although paying some attention to the theory that cooked food is not generally attended with the same benefit to ruminating as to other animals, was evidently almost convinced that those which contained an abundance of starch in their constituents must be rendered more nutritious when exposed to the action of heat.

Potatoes fed in a raw state to stock are laxative in their effects, and are often given to horses as a medicine in cases of "hidebound" with decided benefit. Bots, which have been known to live twenty-four hours immersed in spirits of turpentine, die almost instantly when placed in potato-juice; hence a common practice with horsemen, where bots are suspected, is to first administer milk and molasses to decoy the parasites from the coating of the stomach, and then drench the animal with the expressed juice of potatoes. A decoction made by boiling the parings of potatoes in a small quantity of water is often used as a wash to kill vermin on cattle. Raw potatoes, fed occasionally and in small quantities, are a good tonic for stock of any kind which is kept principally on hay; but all experiments show that when the potato is used for fattening purposes, the tubers should in some way be cooked, that the animal to which they are fed may derive from them the greatest possible amount of nutriment. Repeated experiments demonstrate the fact that horned cattle or hogs lay on as much fat from the consumption of two thirds of a given quantity of potatoes properly cooked as they will by eating the entire quantity in a raw state. In point of nutriment as cattle-food, two pounds of potatoes are considered equivalent to one pound of hay.

HOW TO COOK THE POTATO.

FURNISHED BY

PROF. PIERRE BLOT, OF BROOKLYN.

At the suggestion of a number of friends, I addressed the following note to Professor Blot, which, with his reply, is appended:

PROFESSOR PIERRE BLOT: NEW-YORK, Feb. 15, 1870.

DEAR SIR: In connection with a Prize Essay on the cultivation of the potato, I wish to publish an article on COOKING THE POTATO, to be taken from your *Hand-Book of Practical Cookery.* I write this note to ask whether I can do this with your entire approval. Hoping that such article may aid our American housekeepers to prepare the potato for the table in a more palatable and wholesome manner, I remain yours very truly,

W. T. WYLIE.

BROOKLYN, CENTRAL KITCHEN, Feb. 15, 1870.

REV. W. T. WYLIE:

DEAR SIR: **You are authorized, with the greatest pleasure.** P. BLOT.

In accordance with the above authority, the following selections have been made from the book named:

To Select.—As a general rule, the smaller the eye the better the potatoes. By cutting off a piece from the larger end, you ascertain if they are sound; they must be white, reddish, bluish, etc., according to the species. If spotted, they are not sound, and therefore very inferior. There are several kinds, and all of them are good when sound or coming from a proper soil. Use the kind you prefer, or those that are better fit for the way they are intended to be served.

To Boil. — Being naturally watery, potatoes should never be cooked by boiling except when wanted very white, as for *croquettes.* When boiled whole, put them of an even size as much as possible, in order to cook them evenly. They are better, more mealy, when steamed or baked; but those who have no steamer must, of course, boil them. Cover them with cold water, set on the fire and boil till done, then pour off all the water, put the pan back on a slow fire for five minutes and well covered; then use the potatoes.

To Steam.—Place them above a kettle of boiling water, in a kind of drainer made for that purpose, and adapted to the kettle. The drainer must be covered tight. They cook as fast as by boiling, the degree of heat being the same. When steamed the skin is very easily removed.

To Prepare.—If they are to be boiled, or steamed, or baked, it is only necessary to wash them. If wanted peeled, as for frying, etc., then commence by cutting off the germs or eyes; if young and tender, take the skin off with a scrubbing-brush, and drop immediately in cold water to keep them white; if old, scrape the skin off with a knife, for the part immediately under the skin contains more nutriment than the middle, and drop in cold water also. If wanted cut, either in dice, or like carpels of oranges, or any other way, cut them above a bowl of cold water, so that they drop into it; for if kept exposed to the air, they turn reddish and lose their nutritive qualities.

A l'Allemande.—Steam, peel, and slice the potatoes. Cut some bread in thin slices, and fry bread and potatoes with a little butter, and turn the whole in a bowl, dust well with sugar, pour a little milk all over, and bake for about fifteen minutes; serve warm.

A l'Anglaise.—Steam or boil about a quart of potatoes, and then peel and slice them. Put two ounces of butter in a frying-pan on the fire, and put the potatoes in when melted, toss them for about ten minutes, add salt, pepper, a little grated nutmeg, and serve hot.

Broiled.—Steam, peel, and slice the potatoes. Lay the slices on a gridiron, and place it over a rather slow fire; have melted butter, and spread some over the slices of potatoes with a brush; as soon as the under part is broiled, turn each slice over and spread butter over the other side. When done, dish, salt, and serve them hot. A little butter may be added when dished, according to taste.

Fried.—To be fried, the potatoes are cut either with a vegetable spoon, in fillets, in slices, with a scalloped knife, or with an ordinary one, or cut in pieces like carpels of oranges, or even in dice. When cut, drain and wipe them dry. This must be done quickly, so as not to allow the potatoes to turn reddish. Have a coarse towel ready, then turn the potatoes into a colander, and immediately turn them in the towel, shake them a little, and quickly drop them in hot fat. When done, turn them into a colander, sprinkle salt on them, and serve hot. Bear in mind that fried potatoes must be eaten as hot as possible. Fry only one size at a time, as it takes three times as long to fry them when cut in pieces as when sliced or cut in fillets.

To fry them light or swelled.—When fried, turn into the colander, and have the fat over a brisk fire; leave the potatoes in the colander only about half a minute, then put them back in the very hot fat, stir for about one minute, and put them again in the colander, salt them, and serve hot. If the fat is very hot, when dropped into it for the second time they will certainly swell; there is no other way known to do it. It is as easily done as it is simple. Potatoes cut in fillets and fried are sometimes called *à la Parisienne;* when cut in slices or with a vegetable spoon, they are called *à la française.*

Potatoes cut with a vegetable spoon and fried, make a good as well as a

sightly decoration for a dish of meat or of fish. They may be fried in oil also, but it is more expensive than in fat. They may be fried in butter also, but it is still more expensive than oil, and is not better than fat; no matter what kind of fat is used, be it lard, beef suet, or skimmings of sauces and gravy, it can not be tasted.

Lyonnaise.—Potatoes *Lyonnaise* are prepared according to taste, that is, as much onion as liked is used, either in slices or chopped. If you have not any cold potatoes, steam or boil some, let them cool, and peel and slice them. For about a quart of potatoes, put two ounces of butter in a frying-pan on the fire, and when melted put as much onion as you please, either sliced or chopped, into the pan, and fry it till about half done, when add the potatoes and again two ounces of butter; salt, pepper, and stir and toss gently till the potatoes are all fried of a fine, light-brown color. It may require more butter, as no vegetable absorbs more than potatoes.

Mashed.—Peel and quarter about three pints of potatoes, as directed; put them in a saucepan with more water than is necessary to cover them, and a little salt; set on the fire and boil gently till done, drain, put them back in the saucepan, mash them well and mix them with two ounces of butter, two yolks of eggs, salt, pepper, and milk enough to make them of a proper thickness. Set on the fire for two or three minutes, stirring the while, and serve warm. When on the dish, smooth them with the back of a knife or scallop them, according to fancy.

Mashed and Baked.—Put two ounces of butter in a stewpan and set it on the fire; when hot, add a tea spoonful of parsley chopped fine, and a little salt; five minutes after, put in it a quart of potatoes, prepared, cooked, peeled, and mashed, as directed; then pour on the whole, little by little, stirring continually with a wooden spoon, a pint of good milk; and when the whole is well mixed, and becoming rather thick, take from the fire, place on the dish, then set in a brisk oven for five minutes, and serve.

Sautees.—Take a quart of young and

tender potatoes, peel them with a brush, and cut in slices. Put two ounces of butter in a frying-pan on a quick fire; when hot, put the potatoes in, and fry them till of a golden color ; place them on a dish without any butter, sprinkle chopped parsley and salt on, and serve. They may also be served without parsley, according to taste.

Soufflees.—Steam a quart of potatoes, then peel and mash them in a saucepan and mix an ounce of butter with them ; set on the fire, pour into it, little by little, stirring the while, about half a pint of milk, stir a little longer after the milk is in and until they are turning rather thick ; dish the potatoes, smooth or scallop them with the back of a knife, and put them in a quick oven till of a proper color, and serve.

In Cakes.—Prepare and cook by steam a quart and a half of potatoes, peel and mash them ; mix with them the yolks of five eggs, half a lemon-rind grated, and four ounces of fine white sugar. Put four ounces of butter in a stew-pan and set it on the fire ; when melted, put the mixture in, stirring it with a wooden spoon continually ; as soon as it is in the stew-pan, add the whites of the five eggs, well beaten ; leave on the fire only the time necessary to mix the whole well together, and take off; when nearly cold, add, if handy, and while stirring, a few drops of orange-flower water ; it gives a very good flavor ; then put the whole in a tin mould greased a little with butter ; place in a quick oven for about thirty-five minutes, and serve.

With Butter, or English Fashion.—Put water on the fire with considerable salt in it ; at the first boil, drop a quart of washed potatoes in and boil till

done, when take off, peel, and put them whole in a saucepan, with butter, salt, pepper, and a little nutmeg ; set on a rather slow fire, stirring gently now and then till they have absorbed all the butter. Serve warm. They absorb a great deal of butter.

With Bacon or Salt Pork.—Peel and quarter about a quart of potatoes. Set a saucepan on the fire with about four ounces of fat salt pork cut in dice in it. When fried, put the potatoes in. Season with a bunch of seasonings composed of two sprigs of parsley, one of thyme, and a bay-leaf; salt and pepper to taste, and about half a pint of broth or water. Boil gently till cooked, remove the bunch of seasonings ; skim off the fat, if any, and serve warm. It is served at breakfast, as well as *entremets* for dinner.

With Cream or Milk.—Peel and mash a quart of potatoes, when prepared and cooked. Put two ounces of butter in a stewpan and set it on a good fire ; when melted, sprinkle in it a tea-spoonful of flour, same of chopped parsley, a pinch of grated nutmeg, and salt ; stir with a wooden spoon five minutes ; then add the potatoes, and half a pint of milk or cream ; keep stirring ten minutes longer, take from the fire, sprinkle in them half a table-spoonful of sugar, and serve as warm as possible.

With White Sauce.—Clean, wash, and throw a quart of potatoes in boiling water, with a sprig of thyme, two onions, a bay-leaf, two sprigs of sweet basil, two cloves, salt, and pepper, ; when cooked, take the potatoes out carefully, peel and cut them in two, place them on a warm dish, pour on them a white sauce, and serve warm.

THE POTATO:

ILLUSTRATIONS AND DESCRIPTIONS.

WE propose to add a few pages of illustrations of the new varieties, together with descriptions of the same. A number of these were given in the pamphlet issued last year, and are reproduced from that. In case a new edition is called for, it is likely that a number of additional cuts will be added to it.

We would call attention to the report of a series of experiments which have been made on the farms connected with the Agricultural College of Pennsylvania.

There are very many questions connected with the cultivation of the potato which can be answered satisfactorily only by careful and repeated experiments.

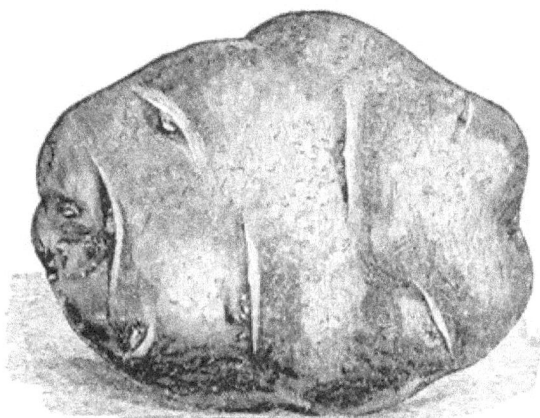

Excelsior.

Seedling of Early Goodrich, now six years old, and is claimed to combine more good qualities than any other potato. D. S. Heffron, of Utica, originated it. Is said to be productive, early, and of good keeping qualities.

MASSASOIT.—A new variety from Western Massachusetts, resembling the Harison in appearance, but earlier and of much better quality; flesh white, cooks dry and mealy, and altogether a superior variety; strongly recommended for a general crop. (See next page.)

REV. W. T. WYLIE:

DEAR SIR: I inclose an extract from the report, suitable, I think, for the pamphlet.

H. N. McALLISTER.

AGRICULTURAL COLLEGE OF PENNSYLVANIA.

From an interesting and instructive report of the Professor of Agriculture to the Board of Trustees of the Agricultural College of Pennsylvania, for 1869, in relation to the results of experiments made upon the three several experimental farms connected with that institution, we make the following extracts touching the Potato, verifying and illustrating some of the principles set forth in the above essay:

1st.—Varieties.

Of upward of thirty different varieties experimented upon, the Early Goodrich, Early Rose, and Harrison are among the best and most prolific.

LIKE WEIGHTS OF SEED UPON EQUAL AREAS OF GROUND.

2d.—Different Modes of Preparing the Seed.

CENTRAL FARM.—One fourth of Plot No. 11—Early Goodrich—*cut tubers*, yields 500 pounds, equal to 286 bushels per acre; *large and whole tubers*, yields 410 pounds, equal to 234 bushels per acre; *medium-sized tubers*, yields 419 pounds, equal to 239 bushels per acre; and *small tubers*, yields 486 pounds, equal to 278 bushels per acre.

3d.—Combined Diversity between Soil and Sub-soil and Common Plowing.

CENTRAL FARM.—The 4 plots, Nos. 11, 16, 116, and 416—*soil and sub-soil plowing*—yields 6200 pounds, equal to 221 bushels per acre; the 2 plots, Nos. 216 and 316—*common plowing*—yields 1845 pounds, equal to but 131 bushels per acre.

4th.—Diversity between Letting all Sprouts Grow and Thinning to Three in each Hill.

EASTERN FARM.—Plot No. 208: Monitors; large and whole tubers, 21½ pounds; *not thinned*; Moro Philips's superphosphate: yield 1174 pounds, equal to 168 bushels per acre.

Plot No. 209: Monitors; large and whole tubers, 23 pounds; *thinned*; Moro Philips's superphosphate; yield 1042 pounds, equal to 149 bushels per acre.

Plot No. 210: Monitors; large and whole tubers, 15 pounds; *not thinned*; stable manure; yield 860 pounds, equal to 124 bushels per acre.

Plot No. 211: Monitors; large and whole tubers, 14½ pounds; *thinned*; stable manure; yield 839 pounds, equal to 119 bushels per acre.

5th.—Diversity from Time of Cutting the Seed-Potatoes.

Plot No. 222: Monitors; *cut two weeks before planting*; yield 580 pounds, equal to 83 bushels per acre.

Plot 223: Monitors; *cut at time of planting*; yield 819 pounds, equal to 117 bushels per acre.

Plot 220: Early Shaw; *cut two weeks before planting*; yield 764 pounds, equal to 100 bushels per acre.

Plot 221: Early Shaw; *cut at time of planting*; yield 907 pounds, equal to 129 bushels per acre.

Massasoit.

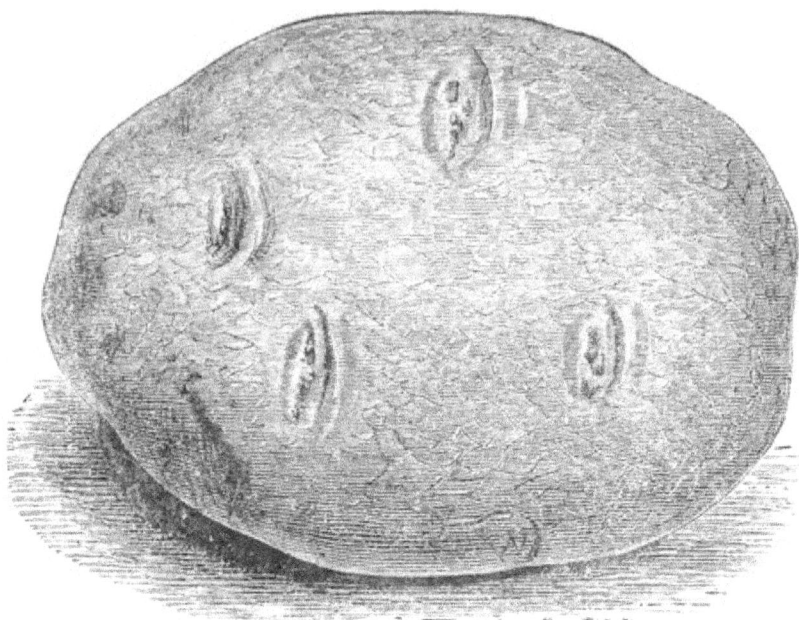

Bresee's Peerless, or No. 6.

THE latest and best of all Mr. Bresee's seedlings for the main crop. This is also a seedling of the Garnet Chili, and originated from the same seed-ball as the Early Rose; skin dull white, occasionally russeted; eyes shallow, oblong; flesh white, mealy; grows to a large size, often weighing from one and a half to two pounds, and enormously productive. At a trial before a committee of the Massachusetts Horticultural Society, in September last, this variety obtained more votes as to quality than any other of Bresee's seedlings.

TABLE OF EXPERIMENTS.

TRY IT AND REPORT RESULTS.

lbs.

Two pounds large-sized potatoes, planted whole				....	∞
"	"	"	"	cut into quarters	∞
"	"	"	"	cut to single eyes	∞
"	"	"	"	cut to single eyes and planted four in a hill ...	∞
"	"	"	"	planted in drills, fifteen inches between the sets,	∞
Two pounds small potatoes, planted whole				....	∞
"	"	"	cut in two pieces		∞
Two pounds cut to single eye, and worked in ridges				....	∞
"	"	"	the surface kept flat	....	∞

To these add such other experiments as may be interesting to you. *Weigh* the product of each carefully, and report *weight, average, size* of each lot, and *quality.*

33

Brezee's King of the Earlies.

Raised, in 1862, by Albert Brezee, of Hubbardton, Vt., from a ball of the Garnet Chili. Vines of medium height, or a little less, and bearing no balls; leaves large; tubers large and handsome, roundish and slightly flattened; eyes small, and somewhat pinkish; skin flesh-colored, or dull pinkish white; flesh white, cooks well, and is of the best quality for the table. Has proven thus far very hardy. The variety will not be sent out until the spring of 1870.

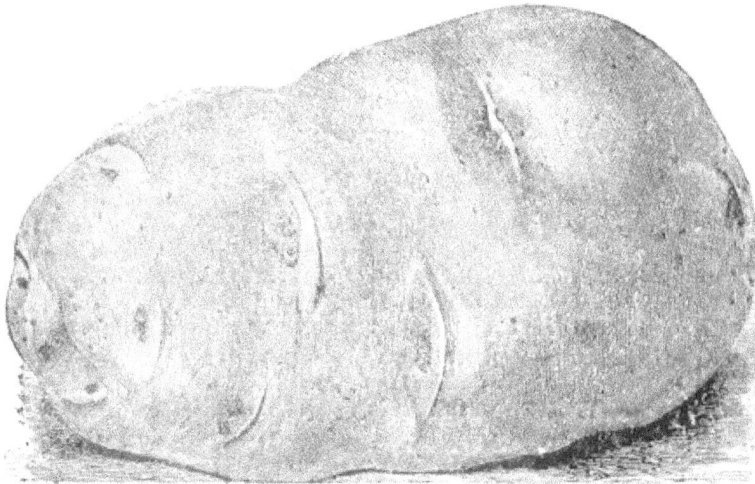

THE EARLY MOHAWK POTATO.

Originated in Michigan, in 1866, from a cross of the Peachblow and Brick Eye. It is of oblong, roundish shape, flattened at the ends. Skin light pink, with pink blush near the eye. Eyes slightly sunken, flesh white, cooks dry and mealy, and of superior flavor. Ripens from six to ten days earlier than the Rose, of uniform large size and but few small ones, and perfectly free from Core or Hollow Heart, and a superior Winter and Spring variety.

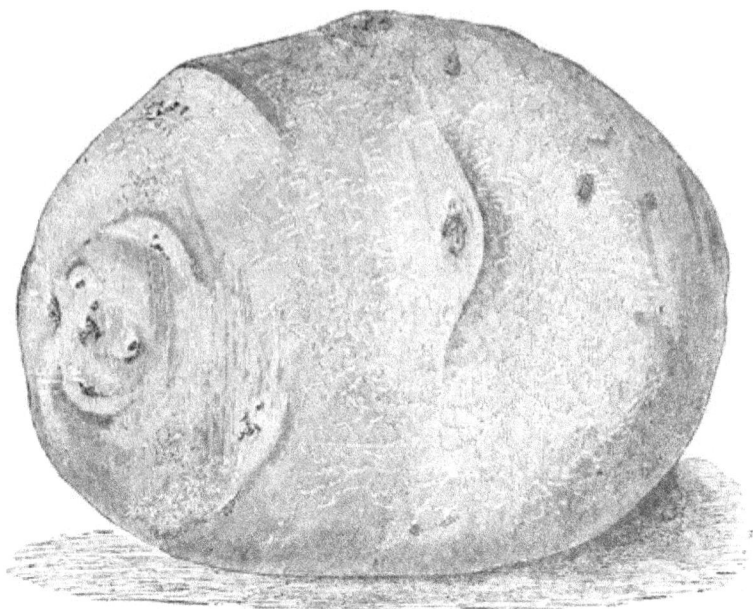

Brezee's Prolific.

This variety originated with Albert Brezee, Esq., of Hubbardton, Vt., in 1861. Mr. Brezee was the originator of the Early Rose, the seed producing both that and Brezee's Prolific being from the same seed-ball, and both are seedlings of the Garnet Chili.

The vines of Brezee's Prolific are of medium height, quite bushy, and somewhat spreading, and with very large leaves; as yet they have produced no seed-balls. Tubers large, regular in shape, and very smooth, slightly oblong, and very much flattened; skin dull white, inclined to be russeted; eyes but little depressed and slightly pinkish; flesh white, rarely if ever hollow; cooks quickly, and is very mealy and of excellent quality. Yield very large, maturing three weeks later than the Early Rose.

Rules Worth Observing.—An experienced cultivator says, "My experience leads me to lay down the following as *safe rules :*

"I. As early as possible, *lay your plans* for the next season's planting, and manure and work your ground accordingly, in advance.

"II. Secure the *best seed,* even if it cost you two or five times as much as a common and less valuable sort.

"III. *Always* get a new, improved variety, as soon as it has been tested and proved. *Remember* the profit is mainly made by the early cultivators. When it gets so common that *you* can buy cheap, you will have to *sell* cheap, too.

"IV. Buy only from reliable dealers, and *be sure* you get the *genuine* article.

"V. Buy, or at least ORDER, if you possibly can, in the fall or winter; you thus save the spring rise of prices.

"VI. Liberal outlay for *seed, manure, tools, and work* gives ten-fold the largest return in money, as well as satisfaction."

15

THE GLEASON.

Also a seedling of 1860, of the Pink Eye Rusty Coat, No. 15, which it closely resembles. When two years old, Mr. Goodrich described it thus : " Longish, rusty, coppery ; leaves and vines dark green ; flowers white ; a very hopeful sort." September 29th, 1863, at digging time, he added : "Very nice ; many in the hill ; no disease." The two seasons, 1865 and 1866, under Dr. Gray's cultivation, this variety yielded at the rate of four hundred bushels to the acre, being more productive than the parent. This variety gives the best satisfaction. The tubrse are not overgrown, but numerous ; have fine-grained, solid flesh, that cooks white. For winter use this kind is excellent. It is a good keeper, and has a fine, rich flavor, especially when baked.

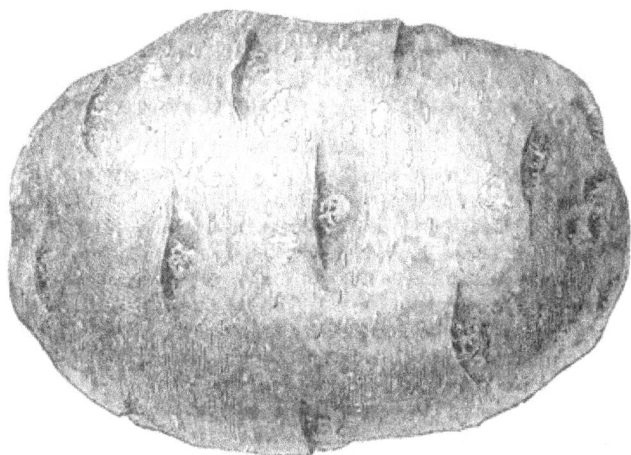

Willard.

J. J. H. Gregory says of this potato : " The Willard is a seedling from the Early Goodrich. It proves to be a half early variety, enormously productive, and is a potato of good promise. It is of a rich rose color, spotted and splashed with white. The flesh is white "

THE EARLY ROSE.

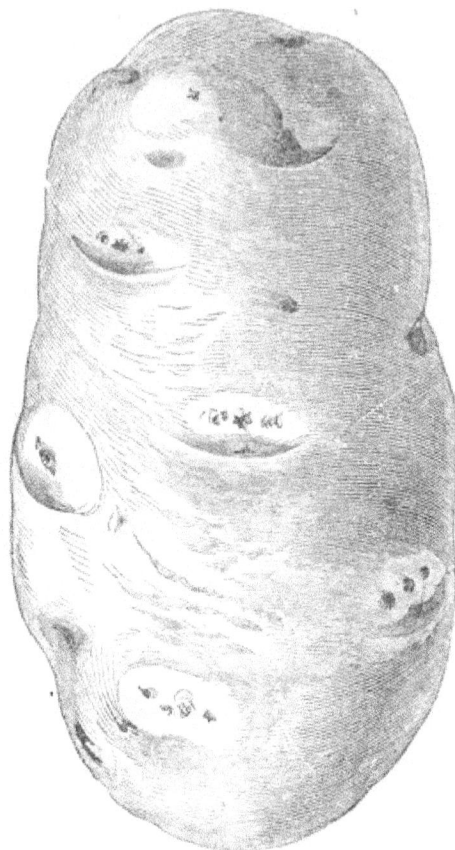

"It is a seedling of the Garnet Chili, that was originated in 1861, by Albert Brezee, Esq., an intelligent farmer of Hortonville, Vt. I have experimented with it for three years, and have been so well pleased with it that I have purchased all Mr. Brezee could spare for the last two years, and have engaged the whole of his small crop for another year.

"It has a stout, erect stalk, of medium height; large leaves; flowers freely; bears no fruit. The tuber is quite smooth, nearly cylindrical, varying to flattish at the centre, tapering gradually toward each end. Eyes shallow, but sharp and strongly marked. Skin thin, tough, of a dull bluish color. Flesh white, solid, and brittle; rarely hollow; boils through quickly; is very mealy, and of the best table quality. It is as healthy and productive as the Early Goodrich, matures about ten days earlier, and is its superior for the table. The cut is a good outline of this beautiful and excellent sort.

"I consider it the most promising very early potato with which I am acquainted, and I have tried nearly all the early sorts of the country.'

How to Double Your Crop, when you have New and Rare Kinds.—In an ordinary hot-bed or cold frame, put some six inches of good, loose, rich soil; split your potato, and lay it cut side down about three inches under the surface. When the sprouts are four or five inches high, lift the potato, slip off the sprouts, and plant them.

You can then cut the tuber into single eyes, and plant as usual. The crop from the sprouts will ripen two weeks before the others. I made $40 this year by trying this with a *handful* of potatoes. Every reader is welcome to it, and may make as much or more than I did, if he secures a few pounds of the newer and costly but valuable kinds.   W.

Early Goodrich.

A seedling of the Cusco of 1860. In 1862, Mr. Goodrich described it: " Round to longish ; sometimes a crease at the insertion of the root ; white ; flowers bright lilac ; (produces) many balls ; yield large. Table quality is already very good. This sort is No. 1 every way."

He said to me in the spring of 1864 : " This early sort gives me more satisfaction than any other I have ever grown." This variety ripens as early as the Ashleaf Kidney ; on rich soil yields from 250 to 350 bushels per acre ; has never shown any disease ; is white-fleshed, and of superior quality.

The above description by D. S. Heffron is fully sustained by my experience.

I noticed at dinner to-day, (Nov. 17th,) every potato in a large dishful had cracked its skin, and from most of them the skin had peeled itself half off.   W.

Rev. W. F. Dixon, of Pine Grove, gives the results of his experience in the following note :

" PINE GROVE, MERCER CO., PA., } September 20, 1868. }

" A year ago last spring, a friend gave me three early Goodrich potatoes, which I planted four eyes in a hill, and last fall I raised over one bushel. I had the Buckeye planted in the same lot. The Goodrich produced about four times as much to the hill as the Buckeye."

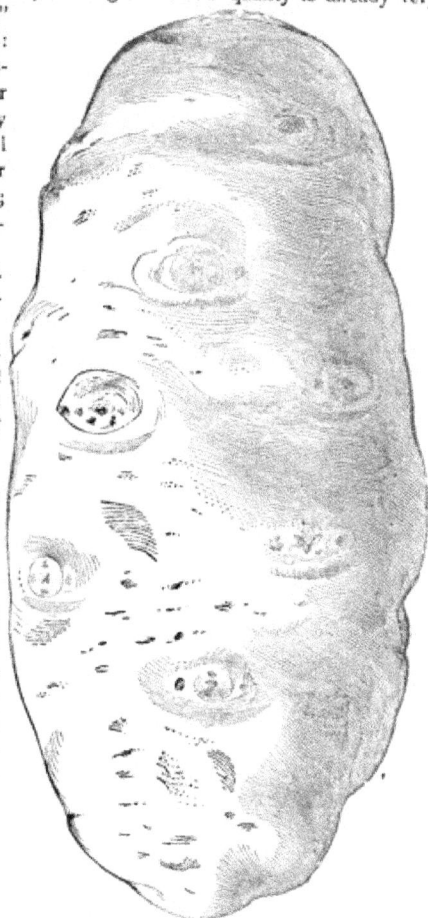

Our country may well honor the memory of Rev. C. E. Goodrich, who, by persevering experiments and patient toil, has produced such wonderful results. His success should stimulate every farmer to make a similar line of experiments.

Potato Crop of New York State.—The total potato crop of the State of New York, this year, is about 25,000,000 bushels. The six great potato counties are Washington, Rensselaer, Saratoga, Monroe, St. Lawrence, and Genesee. Only one other county (Oneida) produces 300,000 bushels ; three others, 600,000 ; one, 500,000 ; six, 400,000. New York county returns a crop of 1700 bushels. The entire crop of the State, 25,000,000 bushels, is raised on 254,403 acres of land. The three counties in the State which produce the most potatoes join each other, viz., Washington, Rensselaer, and Saratoga—their aggregate production reaching within a fraction of 2,500,000 bushels, or more than one-eighth of the total product of the whole State.—*New York Observer.*

HARISON.

MR. HEFFRON gives the following account of this variety: "It is a brother of the Early Goodrich—a seedling of the Cusco of 1860. When two years old, Mr. Goodrich described it thus: 'White, large, not so deep eyes as the parent, nice.'" In 1863, Mr. Goodrich had eleven and a half bushels; and though it was a bad year for disease, and this a young and tender seedling, when he overhauled his seedlings, January 29th, 1864, he made this entry in his book: "All perfect, fine."

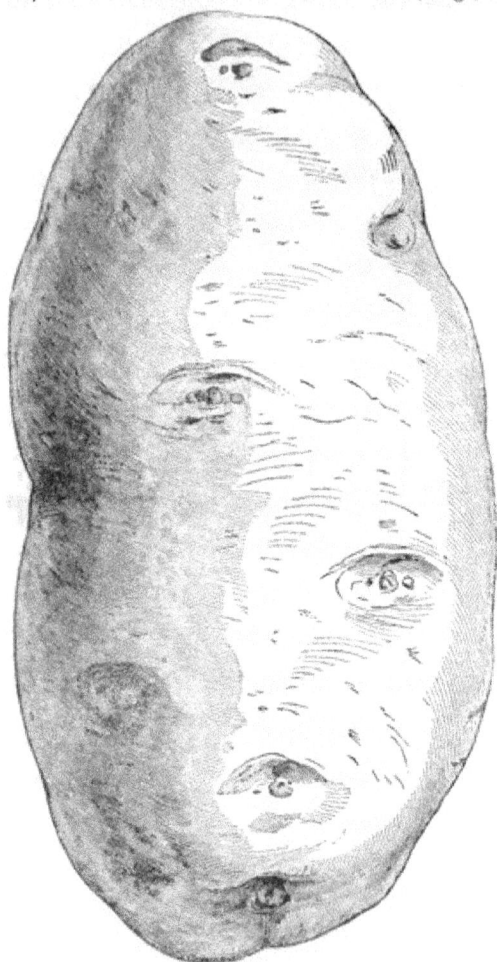

It has a smooth white skin, white flesh, and is the most solid of large potatoes, having no hollow at the centre. It is enormously productive, yielding as well as the parent Cusco, and exceeds all others; its form is good, table quality excellent; keeps well; ripens ten days earlier than the Garnet Chili, and thus far is as hardy as the Garnet Chili.

Among winter sorts this potato must soon hold as high a place as is conceded to the Early Goodrich among the early sorts.

To Keep Potatoes during Winter.—As soon as dry after digging, pick up and handle carefully; store in a dry, well-aired, cool cellar, free from frost, either in bins raised a little from the bottom of the cellar, or in barrels having at least two holes bored through the staves near the bottom, and lay the top head on, over a lath, so as to exclude the light without preventing a free circulation of air. Also sprinkle among the potatoes about half a pint of recently slacked quick-lime to each barrel. If bins are used, cover them over sufficiently to exclude the most of the light. Air the cellar all winter, as often as the temperature outside will admit of it.

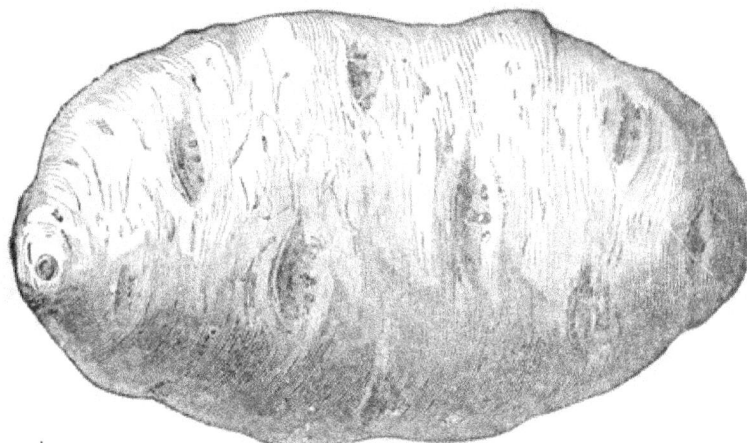

It has a stout, erect stalk, of full medium height, internodes of medium length, and very large leaves ; the tuber is above medium in size, quite smooth, in form of a short cylinder swelled out at the centre, occasionally slightly flattened, and terminating rather abruptly ; eyes shallow, sharp, sometimes swelled out or projecting, and always strongly defined ; skin medium thickness, considerably netted or russet, tough, white ; flesh entirely white, solid, heavy, brittle, and never hollow, and it boils through quickly, with no hard core at centre or stem, is mealy, of floury whiteness, and of superior table quality.

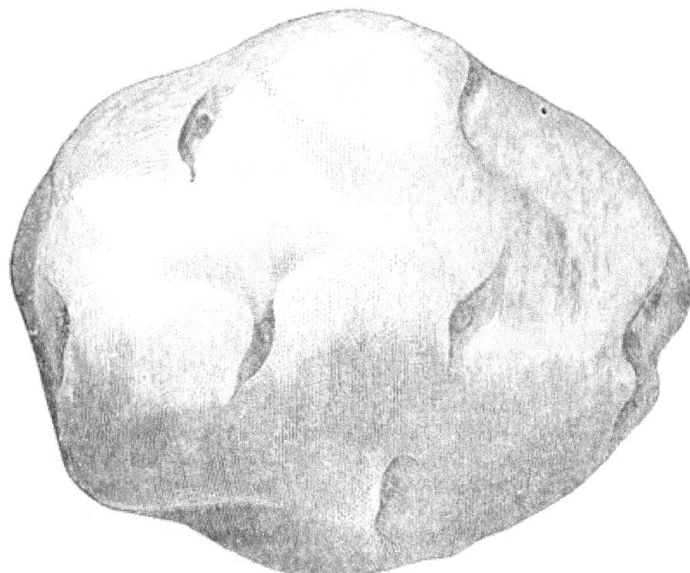

Early Prince.

THE *Early Prince* is a seedling of the Early York, and was propagated in 1864 It has proved to be from a week to ten days earlier than the Early Rose, as far as size and solidity are concerned, and from two to three weeks earlier in quality.